I0622465

THE ANGELS OF THE SEVEN CHURCHES

THE ANGELS OF THE SEVEN CHURCHES

MARIE SMITH

ARPress
ILLUMINATING IDEAS
EMPOWERING VOICES

Copyright © 2022 by Marie Smith

All rights reserved. No part of this publication may be reproduced, distributed, or transmitted in any form or by any means, including photocopying, recording, or other electronic or mechanical methods, without prior written permission of the publisher, except in the case of brief quotations embodied in critical reviews and certain other noncommercial uses permitted by copyright law. For permission requests, write to the publisher, addressed "Attention: Permissions Coordinator," at the address below.

ARPress
45 Dan Road Suite 36
Canton MA 02021

Hotline: 1(800) 220-7660
Fax: 1(855) 752-6001

Ordering Information:
Quantity Sales. Special discounts are available on quantity purchases by corporations, associations, and others. For details, contact the publisher at the address above.

Printed in the United States of America.

ISBN-13	Paperback	979-8-9899505-4-6
	eBook	979-8-9899505-5-3
	Hardback	979-8-9899505-6-0

Library of Congress Control Number: 2024904626

CONTENTS

The Angels of the Seven Churches

The mystery of the seven stars which thou saw in my right hand and the seven golden candlesticks. The seven stars are the angels of the seven churches: and the candlesticks which thou saw are the seven churches. (Revelation 1: 20, NKJV, The Holy Bible).

The Letters to the Churches.

When you read Revelation chapters 2 and 3, it is essential to see four functions of the letters.

Each letter was given to the seven churches as initially addressed. And these churches were in existence in Asia at the time of the revelation. Many other churches existed in Asia simultaneously, but the churches selected were representative of the spiritual conditions that existed at that time.

The letter can also be used in history. According to the account, the Church has passed through eras like that described in each of the seven churches.

These letters can be applied to our current churches of today. These unique letters were written to the individual churches in Asia, but the same strengths and weaknesses can now be found in today's Body of Christ Churches.

Each of us can utilize the letters on an individual foundation. Look at the notes for each church during that time and ask yourself how we measure up individually today.

These letters were written by John in roughly 94 - 96 A.D. when the Church of Jesus Christ was a little over 60 years old. The church had experienced incredible growth in the face of severe persecution.

Under the rule of Rome, records show over 45,000 Christians were slain by crucifixion, burned to death, and thrown to wild animals. In increasing, corruption was springing up in the Church.

When John wrote the letters to the seven churches, many believers were afraid about the uncertain future.

They were afraid of being strong enough to stand up to adversities that they would be facing and if they could endure the persecution. To these early Christians, Jesus gave his end-time plan through these letters.

The seven churches of Revelation

The churches of seven cities (Rev. 1:11) were recipients of an apocalyptic letter from God, which John was called to write while he was exiled on the island of Patmos. By honor, rebuke, and warning, the people of God were encouraged to remain faithful in adversity. These churches held significant roles in the Christian experience of Asia Minor as a result of their location within a transportation network linking different parts of the region.

INTRODUCTION

Some Christian shepherds are in rebellion against God; they have fallen from grace and are walking in the sin of witchcraft because they are in rebellion against God. They have become stiff neck, unreasonably obstinate, or set in their purpose and opinion. Then they started to challenge God's Word as they began to mix the doctrine, manage the flock to worship them and not worship the Lord. They suppress flock in their care, making them as complex as stone and wood and difficult to shape or work. There is a violation of rights or duty, gross injustice or wickedness, abomination, crime, sexual sins, offense, unrighteousness, wrongdoing, and infamy. Their flock began to give the shepherds reverence instead of giving God reverence; they became blind in their own eyes. What seems right in their mind. Now the flock is idolatrizing the Shepherds. These shepherds began to believe they were right and above God. Now they have become a God to their congregation. Some have become Christian witches as deception set in.

According to the Bible, rebellion is the sin of witchcraft, and stubbornness **is iniquity and idolatry.** Because thou hast rejected the word of the Lord, he hath also rejected thee from being king. (1 Samuel 15: 23, NKJV, Holy Bible).

According to the book of Ezekiel, these shepherds are irresponsible shepherds. And the word of the Lord came to me, saying, Son of man, prophesy against the shepherds of Israel, prophesy and say to them, "Thus says the Lord God to the shepherds: Woe to the shepherds of Israel who feed themselves! Should not the shepherds feed the flocks? You eat the fat and clothe yourselves with the wool; you slaughter the fatlings, but you do not provide for the community. (Ezekiel 34:1-10, NKJV, The Holy Bible).

The weak you have not strengthened, nor have you healed those who were sick, bound up the broken, nor brought back what has driven away, nor sought what was lost: but with force and cruelty, you have ruled them.

So, they were scattered because there was no shepherd: and they became food for all the beasts of the field when they were scattered.

My sheep wandered through all the mountains and on every high hill; yes, my flock was scattered over the whole face of the earth, and no one was seeking or searching for them. (Ezekiel 34:1-10, NKJV, The Holy Bible).

Therefore, you shepherds. Hear the word of the Lord: As I live," says the Lord God, "inevitably because My flocks became a prey, and My congregation became food for every beast of the field: because there was no shepherd, nor did my shepherds search for my flock, but the shepherds fed themselves and did not feed my flock. (Ezekiel 34:1-10, NKJV, The Holy Bible).

Therefore, O shepherds, hear the word of the Lord! Thus says the Lord God: Behold, I am against the shepherds, and I will require My flock at their hand. I will cause them to cease feeding the sheep, and the shepherds shall feed themselves no more; for I will deliver my community from their mouths, that they may no longer be food for them. (Ezekiel 34:1-10, NKJV, The Holy Bible).

CHAPTER 1

The Loveless Church

To the Church in Ephesus

Rev 2:1 "To the angels of the church in Ephesus write: These are his words who holds the seven stars in his right hand and walks among the seven golden lampstands: Rev 2:2 I know your deeds, your hard work, and your perseverance. I know that you cannot tolerate wicked men, that you have tested those who claim to be apostles but are not and have found them false.

Rev 2:3 You have persevered and have endured hardships for my name and have not grown weary. Rev 2:4 Yet I hold this against you: You have forsaken your first love. Rev 2:5 Remember the height from which you have fallen! Repent and do the things you did at first. If you do not repent, I will come to you and remove your lampstand from its place. Rev 2:6 But you have this in your favor: You hate the practices of the Nicolaitans, which I also hate. Rev 2:7 He who has an ear, let him hear what the Spirit says to the churches.

To him, who overcomes, I will give the right to eat from the tree of life, which is in the paradise of God. (Revelation 2:1-7).

- ❖ **Ephesus:** Apostolic, desirable, they love their first love.
- ❖ **Seven:** Completeness, Perfection
- ❖ **Stars:** Israel, Generations, Nations
- ❖ **Gold:** Kingship, Kingdom Glory, God, or gods
- ❖ **Lampstand:** Candlestick: Represent the Church

Ephesus: The Capital of Asia was the western part of Asia minor. It was colonized principally by Athens (Greece). The spiritual decline of the churches began as deception set in. It was populated mainly by Athens, Asia's first and most significant metropolis. Temples of Diana, who there had her chief shrine; and for its theater, the largest in the world, capable of containing 50,000 spectators. Like all ancient theaters, they are open to the sky. They exhibited the lights of wild beasts and men with animals.

Many Jews took up their residence in this city, and here the seeds of the gospel were sown immediately after Pentecost (Acts 2:9; 6:9). At the close of his second missionary journey (about A.D.51), When Paul returned from Greece to Syria (Acts 18: 18-21), he first visited this city.

He remained, however, for only a short time, as he was hastening to keep the feast, probably of Pentecost at Jerusalem. Still, Paul left Aquila and Priscilla behind him to carry on spreading the Gospel.

During Paul's third missionary journey, he reached Ephesus from the upper coasts (Act 19:1), i.e., from the inland parts of Asia Minor, and Tarried here for about three years. So successful and abundant were his labors that " all they which dwelt in Asia heard the word of the Lord Jesus, both Jews and Greeks (Acts 19: 10). During this period, the seven churches of the Apocalypse were founded not by Paul's labors but by missionaries whom he may have sent out from Ephesus and by the influence of converts returning to their homes.

Paul returned from his journey; Paul touched the city Miletus, 30 miles south of Ephesus (Acts 20:15), and sent for the presbyters of Ephesus to meet him there; he delivered to them with a touching farewell charge which is recorded in (Acts 20: 18-35).

Ephesus is not again mentioned till near the close of Paul's life, when he writes to Timothy, encouraging him to abide still at Ephesus (1 Timothy 1: 3).

The churches of Ephesus ended in a spiritual decline because of deception. They began to have False Apostles. All the people of Ephesus had to do was repent and do their first works over. Sometimes the sin can be so wicked, or the person has fallen from grace that they must do their first works over and repent. We are so stubborn and full of pride. Pride is a high or inordinate opinion of one's dignity, importance, merit, or superiority, whether as cherished in mind or displayed in bearing, conduct, etc.

The state or feeling of being proud. Becoming or dignified sense of what is due to oneself or one's position or character; self-respect; self-esteem. The pleasure or satisfaction is taken in something done by or belonging to oneself or believed to reflect credit upon oneself:

Something that causes a person or persons to be proud: There was no forgiveness or love for the people.

Revelation 2:1 "Unto the angel of the church of Ephesus write, These things saith he that holdout the seven stars in his right hand, who walketh amid the seven golden candlesticks."

"Angel": The elder or pastor from the church (1:16, 20).

"Ephesus": The city of Ephesus was one of the most important commercial and religious cities in Asia Minor. The most famous temple of the goddess (Diana) was located there. It was also John's headquarters before his exile. Ephesus served as the "mother" church to the others, connected by the same Roman road.

There was a literal church of Ephesus. Many believe that this specific church was symbolic of the apostolic age from about (30 to 100 A.D.); it is called the Apostolic Church. After viewing it carefully, we can see some of the churches in our day falling into just this category. Here again, this message is sent to the ministering spirit of this church.

From the spiritual standpoint of churches today, we would see this church located in a very worldly-wise surrounding but being a church holding up a guideline against the evil surroundings. This church would be a spiritual church guided and taught through the Holy Spirit of God. This church will be found working when the Lord comes back. They have been full of the power and presence of God. As we see in the next verse, Jesus first tells them the good, then tells them of their weakness. Even though this church has worked hard and not given up, we see that they have a few faults.

Revelation 2-4: The church is commended because of its soundness of faith and perseverance through persecution. However, its people have come under Christ's discipline for having "left" (not lost) their "first love" or former devotion to Christ.

Revelation 2:2 "I know thy works, and thy labor, and thy patience, and how thou canst not bear them which are evil: and thou hast tried them which say they are apostles and are not, and hast found them, liars:"

Warning: Jesus always starts by telling something good. He commends them for their hard work and patience. To be patient is undoubtedly a virtue that most of us do not possess. This church leader and the people seem to be working for the Lord.

"Them which say they are apostles": The Ephesian church exercised spiritual discernment. It knew how to evaluate men who claimed spiritual leadership by their doctrine and behavior (1 Thess. 5:20-21).

Revelation 2:3 "And hast bore, and hast patience, and for my name's sake hast labored, and hast not fainted."

This spiritual shepherd hates evil. The letter that this shepherd seems to do as the Scripture suggests and tries the spirits to see whether they are of God or not. This church does not just accept everyone who says he is an apostle. They judge the letter before they get the apostle. It seems that this church is well-grounded in the Word. The physical church was one of the older churches founded by Paul and nurtured by Timothy. This physical church of Ephesus was in a busy city.

"Hast not fainted": For over forty years, this church has remained faithful to the Word and the Lord since its founding. For Christ's sake and reputation, the members had endured difficulty and persecution, always driven by the right motive.

Revelation 2:4 "Nevertheless I have [somewhat] against thee, because thou hast left thy first love. "

"Left thy first love": To be a Christian is to love the Lord Jesus Christ (John 14:21, 23; 1 Cor. 16:22). But the Ephesian's zeal and enthusiasm for Christ had become cold, automatic custom. Their doctrinal and moral purity, undiminished passion for the truth, and disciplined service were no alternative to the love for Christ they had forsaken.

2 Timothy 3:5: "Having a form of godliness but denying the power thereof: from such turn away."

Probably this church has gotten too modern for healing and deliverance. Perhaps some of the world's music had crept in unaware. Maybe this church has begun to envision more than teaching. This church is more attractive to the world than to God.

Our first love, if we are believers, is putting Jesus ahead of everything else. This church's problems spiritually can be seen in most of our churches today. God will not allow compromise, but we see just that on every hand.

Revelation 2:5 "Remember therefore from whence thou art fallen, and repent, and do the first works; or else I will come unto thee quickly and remove thy candlestick out of his place, except thou repent."

"Remove thy candlestick": God's judgment would bring an end to the Ephesian church.

There is no replacement for undivided, genuine, undying love for Jesus Christ. Jesus warned the church at Ephesus to "repent, and do the first works; or else, I will come unto thee quickly and remove the candlestick, out of his place, except thou repent." He warned that if they did not repent, judgment would fall. They would no longer be a true light and witness to the world.

Therefore, how many of our churches today are lifeless, dull, and unthinking? How many lack the light and witness of Christ and His power? The condition in this church, and our churches and individual lives, did not happen overnight.

It was a gradual process whereby believers left their "first" love, their passionate "bridal" love for Christ. The "first love" to which Christ called the church in Ephesus to return can be with the "bridal" love in a marriage relationship.

God expects holiness and righteousness of His people, and even more than that, He wants our pure love for Him. If you are going to church for any other reason than to fellowship with God and learn of His will in your life, you must ask yourself this question: Is what I am doing satisfying to God or me?

The wonderful thing about God is that He will allow us to repent. If we repent, He will forgive us and give us another chance. We have an advocate with the Father, Jesus Christ the righteous.

Jesus, in verse above, is telling the physical church at Ephesus and the spiritual church of our day to stop all of the worldly-wise holdings on, and get back to church, like our ancestors. The church must love and reverence God. Just as Moses was told to remove his shoes because he was on Holy Ground, we must realize that we too are on Holy ground in God's presence.

The things of the Spirit are from God as a gift. They cannot and should not be taught. The items of the Spirit are not received because we have figured out a way to make God give them to us. We welcome them as a gift from God because we are humble enough to receive them. Nothing is more remarkable than for the Spirit of God to move in His church. The advantages of the Spirit are to be sought from God but not to be used for our purposes. God still heals. God still saves. God still raises the dead. God still delivers the oppressed. God does it; the power is His. We may be the instrument He uses, but it is not our power; it is His. (Songs of Solomon)

A new bride is so in love with her husband that he is the central focus of her life. When she takes her wedding vows, she promises to forsake all others and give herself solely to him. She eagerly anticipates his desires and lovingly tries to meet all his needs. She spends every possible moment with him. In this "bridal love" relationship, a unique intimacy develops between the bride and her bridegroom. (Songs of Solomon)

She longs to know everything possible about him. She opens her heart to him, revealing her innermost secrets and desires. While they are apart, she longs for him and eagerly anticipates when she will be with him once again. Because of her love, the bride puts her bridegroom first, before all else, including her own needs, desires, and ambitions. (Songs of Solomon)

We can have a pure, genuine, self-sacrificing "bridal love" for Christ that makes the believers willing to give themselves 100% for Christ. It is a love that burned up their selfish desires, motivated them to serve Christ with single-hearted devotion, and made them willing to lay down their lives for the cause of Christ.

Christ's love is a love you cannot explain that we must have a fire within us to enable us to fulfill the purposes of God in these final minutes before Christ's return. Just as Christ called the church in Ephesus to return to their first love, He is walking among us today, calling us to repent and return to our first love.

Here are seven warning signs that signal that a church or individual has left their first love.

- Christ is no longer the central focus of your life
- You neglect your relationship with the Lord and spend less time in prayer, worship, and the Word
- You allow family, friends, job, and your desires to come between you and your relationship with God
- There is a loss of intimacy in your relationship with God
- You are caught in a cycle of dead works
- You are more tolerant of sin
- You will no longer have a burning passion for the lost.

Our works are inspired by intense love and devotion to the Lord. Relate your passion for the Lord today with what it was then. Has your love grown deeper, or has it lost its fervency? Does an affectionate love for God inspire your works, or are you doing them simply out of a feeling of duty? Ask the Lord to forgive you for leaving your first love. Begin to do your first work again. Make a new commitment to the basics of prayer, worship, and the Word.

Fan the flame of the dying embers of your first love through renewed communion with the Lord. This sincere love is required of all those who belong to the Lord. Jesus called this the first and great commandment:

"Thou shalt love the Lord thy God with all thy heart, and with all thy soul, and all thy mind." "This is the first and great commandment." (Matt. 22:37-38).

The worst thing in all the world would be to have walked closely with God and lose out with God because of compromise and worldliness.

We read in this verse, if this is the condition of you or your church, **REPENT:** Jesus, having said this one thing that He has against them, goes immediately back to praising them as we see in the next verse.

Revelation 2:6 "But this thou hast, that thou hate the deeds of the Nicolaitans, which I also hate."

Warning: here that Jesus, like this church, hates the sin and not the sinner. The deeds are hated, not the doer. There seems to be no record of the Nicolaitans except for this mention here. It is possible to hate evil and still not be living a satisfying life in God's sight. Worldliness is something we must avoid entirely.

Nicaulous and Balaam are in the same category. Probably evil with no specific root. The doctrine of Balaam, Nicaulous, and the Jezebel church thought that being Christians freed them from the moral law. They believed that idolatry and fleshly things would not be held against them because they had been set free by Christ. Some of the moderation we see in the churches today stem from this very belief.

So many are trying to bring Jesus down to our level or elevate us up to His level. It is a dangerous doctrine to make ourselves into gods. That is why Lucifer was thrown out of heaven. Worldliness must not be intermingled with the worship of God. We must not only not participate in this but hate this practice.

Revelation 2:7 "He that hath an ear, let him hear what the Spirit saith unto the churches; To him that overcomes will I give to eat of the tree of life, which is in the midst of the paradise of God."

We all have ears, but this is speaking of that inner ear of the heart that receives the truth. Therefore, that Spirit is taken advantage of, meaning God's Spirit. It is not just any spirit but the Holy Spirit of God. We also see here that He is speaking to the churches and suddenly rises to individuals in the church when He says:

"To him that overcomes." According to John's definition, to be an overcomer is to be a Christian (1 John 5:4).

We are not saved jointly but as individuals. We as individuals must decide who we will follow. We notice here also that there is something to overcome. We must overcome licentious temptations of the flesh.

All believers in Jesus will eat of the tree of life. Jesus is the Tree of Life. True believers enjoy the promise of heaven (see notes on 22:2; Gen. 2:9).

God is a Spirit; Jesus is a Spirit who was housed in a body for His stay on earth. We are a spirit, as well, housed in a body. If we are believers, our soul will immediately go to heaven when it leaves our body. The soul will rise at the resurrection and rejoin our spirit. The tree of life is in heaven. Paradise is the garden in heaven. It is a heavenly restoration of the Garden of Eden. The divine being is even more incredible.

One Like a Son of Man

Rev 1:9 I, John, your brother and companion in the suffering and the kingdom and patient endurance that are ours in Jesus, was on the island of Patmos because of the word of God and the testimony of Jesus. Rev 1:10 On the Lord's Day I was in the Spirit, and I heard behind me a loud voice like a trumpet, Rev 1:11 which said: "Write on a scroll what you see and send it to the seven churches: to Ephesus, Smyrna, Pergamum, Thyatira, Sardis, Philadelphia, and Laodicea."

Rev 1:12 I turned around to see the voice speaking to me. And when I turned, I saw seven golden lampstands, Rev 1:13, and among the lampstands was someone "like a son of man," dressed in a robe reaching down to his feet and with a golden sash around his chest. Rev 1:14 His head and hair were white like wool, as white as snow, and his eyes were like blazing fire. Rev 1:15 His feet were like bronze glowing in a furnace, and his voice was like the sound of rushing waters.

Rev 1:16 In his right hand, he held seven stars, and out of his mouth came a sharp double-edged sword. His face was like the sun shining in all its brilliance.

Rev 1:17 When I saw him, I fell at his feet as though dead. Then he placed his right hand on me and said: "Do not be afraid. I am the First and the Last. Rev 1:18 I am the Living One; I was dead, and behold I am alive forever and ever! And I hold the keys of death and Hades.

Rev 1:19 "Write what you have seen, what is now, and what will occur later. Rev 1:20 The mystery of the seven stars that you saw in my right hand and of the seven golden lampstands is this: The seven stars are the angels of the seven churches, and the seven lampstands are the seven churches. (Rev 1:9-20).

CHAPTER 2

The Persecuted Church

And unto the church's angel in Smyrna write, these things saith the first and the last, which was dead, and is alive. (Revelation 2:9 (KJV). I know thy works, tribulation, and poverty (but thou art rich), and I know the blasphemy of them which say they are Jews, and are not, but are the synagogue of Satan. (Revelation 2:10 (KJV)

Fear none of those things which thou shalt suffer: behold, the devil shall cast some of you into prison, that ye may be tried; and ye shall have tribulation ten days: be thou faithful unto death, and I will give thee a crown of life. (Revelation 2:11 (KJV). He hath an ear, let him hear what the Spirit saith unto the churches; He that overcomes shall not be hurt of the second death.

In the city of *Smyrna*: people were martyrdom, persecution, poverty, the devil, and false Jews.

John was told to write down what he saw in a book and to send it to seven churches in the province of Asia (western Asia Minor): Ephesus, Smyrna, Pergamos, Thyatira, Sardis, Philadelphia, and Laodicea (1:11).

The original recipients of Revelation were the believers in these seven churches. Tradition reports that the apostle John exercised spiritual oversight over these churches while he resided at Ephesus during the final decades of the first century. The order of listing the seven churches forms a semicircle beginning in the west at Ephesus, then extending northward to Pergamos, and subsequently southeastward to Laodicea. The revelation was probably sent initially as a circular letter starting at Ephesus and thence throughout the province.

When he was arrested, John was in Ephesus, ministering to the church and surrounding cities. Seeking to strengthen those congregations, he could no longer minister to them in person, following the divine command (1:11).

John addressed Revelation to them (1:4). The churches had begun to feel the effects of persecution; at least one man, probably a pastor, had already been martyred (2:13), and John himself exiled. But the storm of persecution was about to break in full fury upon the seven churches so dear to the apostle's heart (2:10).

To those churches, Revelation provided a message of hope: God is in sovereign control of all the events of human history. Though evil often seems pervasive and wicked men all-powerful, their ultimate doom is certain. Christ will come in glory to judge and rule.

Smyrna": It is 35 miles north of Ephesus. Smyrna was a rich and beautiful commercial city in Asia Minor and recognized by Rome as its loyal supporter and a center of emperor worship. The Lord again commended their good works in His message to this church, "I know your works, tribulation, and poverty." These believers were persecuted and often lost their means of living because of their devotion to the Lord.

Making a public confession of their faith suggested poverty, hunger, imprisonment, and sometimes death. The word "tribulation" is trial, pain, hardship, and misery used here to portray an image of a vast rock crushing whatever lies beneath it. The word express continuous and robust anxiety. Many people are suffering "extreme and persistent pressure." You are not forgotten! Jesus sees and knows.

It is interesting to me that Jesus calls Himself inversely here than at the church of Ephesus. In the Ephesus letter, He says, "He holds the seven stars in his right hand, who walketh amid the seven golden candlesticks." Here at Smyrna, He calls Himself "the first and last, which was dead, alive."

The description here is that this letter is not from the Father or the Holy Spirit but God the Son, Jesus, as we know Him. We see from this that God does not deal the same with everyone. He deals with us at an individual level of our comprehension.

You see in the synagogue in Jerusalem, when Jesus called them "whited walls" (Matthew 23:27), clean on the outside and filthy on the inside. Jesus said, "Woe unto you, scribes and Pharisees, hypocrites!". Jesus called them a generation of vipers (Matthew 23:33).

All those who claim to be Christians are Christians. If we are not careful, we will be like these Jews. We may say we are Christian, and the world might believe that we are because of our outward appearance, but Jesus always looks at the heart.

Matthew 7:22-23 "Many will say to me in that day, Lord, have we not prophesied in thy name? and in thy name have cast out devils? and in thy name done many wonderful works?" "And then will I profess unto them, I never knew you: depart from me, ye that work iniquity." Sometimes Christianity was a front for some selfish motives.

The **repentance** and **salvation** that counts are what goes on in our heart. It is like having a new restored heart placed inside us, washed in the Blood of the Lamb. Being born again means having a brand-new heart and having no longing to sin.

The heart is either dreadfully wicked or clean in Jesus's name. Some call it an altered heart, whatever promise is made in the heart.

❖ When Jesus speaks of His being "*the first and last,*" He is speaking of His Eternal Spirit
❖ When He speaks of "which was dead and is alive," He speaks of His body which was resurrected from the grave.

Jesus knows all; He was moving and is striding amongst the churches. His eyes of fire see everything, even in our hearts. He has nothing but good things to say about this church in Smyrna. To know them is to love them. Jesus knows how hard they have worked for the kingdom. He knows that they are rich in service to Him. They are rich in knowledge of His Word. They have diligently sought Him in His Word. They are rich in the gifts of the Holy Spirit. They have been through incredible hardship. The trial comes to make you strong. They are vital because they have been tried and have not failed God.

Revelation 2:9 "I know thy works, and tribulation, and poverty, (but thou art rich) and I know the blasphemy of them which say they are

Jews, and are not, but are the synagogue of Satan."

"Which say they are Jews": Although they were Jews bodily, they were not faithful Jews but spiritual pagans (Rom. 2:28). People affiliated with other pagans' gods in putting Christians to death as they attempted to stamp out the Christian faith.

"Synagogue of Satan": With the rejection of its Messiah, Judaism is a tool of Satan as emperor worship.

Perhaps, their poverty spoken of here indicates that they are not obsessed with having worldly wealth. Therefore, they worship other pagan gods. They are not rich in things the world would group them as prosperity. Their wealth is of spiritual things. The treasure that we should all be seeking is the treasure stored up in heaven.

If there is a church in this group that we should all want to be like, it would be this church at Smyrna.

This *"Synagogue of Satan"* that comes against them is what we were contemplating before. These are spiritual people with an outward appearance of belief but no inward verdict. This plain church at Smyrna had many martyrs who stood against the evil, idolatrous people around them even unto death.

In our day, it is the identical condition. If we are in God's army, we must be prepared to stand for what is right even unto death. The Spirit and the flesh world will be confined in battle until the return of Jesus.

The world, its organization, and even the idolatrous church contradicted true righteousness and holiness. Jesus is coming back for a church that is without spot or wrinkle.

Revelation 2:10 "Fear none of those things which thou shalt suffer: behold, the devil shall cast some of you into prison, that ye may be tried; and ye shall have tribulation ten days: be thou faithful unto death, and I will give thee a crown of life."

He said they would suffer. He lets them know that He and the Father know all about their suffering. They must stay faithful unto the end, and marvelous rewards will be theirs in heaven. Jesus advises them they will be thrown into prison.

We know from history that these believers were thrown into prison in the plain church of Smyrna. Many in our day are thrown into jail for their faith.

It is becoming tougher and harsher to be a Christian and even more challenging to minister. The church is under assault by the devil.

The meaning of Christ's words to this church that they would have tribulation for "ten days" refers to biblical wars. The Early Church suffered ten primary oppressions under Nero, Domitian, Trajan, Marcus Aurelius, Severus, Maximum, Decius, Valerian, Aurelian, and Diocletian. There were also some notable tortures in the local Smyrna Church, which lasted "ten days." The meaning of this is that their imprisonment will be brief.

It is straightforward to follow Jesus when all is working well. The actual test is, will you stay when all probabilities are against you?

When your friends and relatives have given up, will you stand? If we are faithful and stand, a crown of life awaits us. The crown of life is the one the Lord Himself prepares for us. Crown of life means; "ruling over death." There will be no more death, neither shall there be mourning.

Revelation 21:4-5 "neither sorrow, nor crying, neither shall there be any more pain: for the former things are passed away." "Behold, I make all things new." Many shall be martyred before the return of Christ.

Today, Christ's letter to you during your pain, suffering, persecution, and testing is "Fear Not!" No matter what you are facing, sickness, disease, family problems, or even the possibility of death, do not fear because:

2 Tim. 1:7 "God hath not given us the spirit of fear, but power, love, and a sound mind."

Over and over throughout the Bible, we are instructed by Jesus not to fear. Fear is not of God. Fear is the opposite of faith. We should have confidence in all things.

John 14:1 "Let not your heart be troubled: ye believe in God, also believe in me."

- We are the one who allows fear to come in.
- God wants us to have faith enough to move a mountain (Matthew 17:20).
- The church is under the attack of the devil.
- If your church is not under attack, check and see why not.
- We must be a threat to the enemy before we are attacked.
- So many churches are so penetrated by the world that Satan is not even bothering them.

A church grounded on the accurate Word of God is a threat to Satan and is under terrible attack. One thing that gives us the courage to go on in the face of all of this is the fact that Jesus has won this battle for us on the cross. We need to hang on and receive the victory. Do not throw in the towel or give up.

The devil has power on this earth. He is our enemy. It is a constant battle to overcome him. Just remember that the ability to rebuke him is in the name of Jesus. Jesus is the one who charges; we are His ambassadors. It is straightforward to follow Jesus when everything is running well. The actual test is, will you stay when all probabilities are against you?

When your friends and relatives have given up, will you stand? If we are faithful and stand, a crown of life awaits us. The crown of life is the one the Lord Himself prepares for us. Crown of life means "ruling over death." There will be no more death, neither shall there be grief.

Revelation 2:11 "He that hath an ear, let him hear what the Spirit saith unto the churches; He that overcomes shall not be hurt of the second death. "He that overcomes" identifies every Christian (verse 7).

We hear again, take out the covers in your inner man and receive from God His truths. There is a great promise to the overcomers. The death associated with hell will not happen to them. They have been crowned with everlasting life.

The greatest gift that we could ever obtain is the gift of eternal life with Jesus. To know we would be divided from Jesus for all of eternity would be more hell than I would care to bear. The only life worth having is with Him. I cannot say enough good about this church at Smyrna.

There are only two in the seven that God has no warning. Smyrna is one of them, and the other is Philadelphia. Under great persecution, this

church stands and, having even faced death, still stands.

If you were to explain this church in contemporary English, you would say that the whole Word of God is preached to people who will accept the Truth.

The shepherd teaches the flock the Word of God several times a week. The congregation studies the Scriptures, ever eager to learn more so they can be more and more in the will of God. They are not shaken by winds of false doctrine, for they test everything and everyone against the Scriptures. They have on the whole armor of God. They are filled with the Holy Spirit and operate in the gifts of the Spirit. They realize there is a battle going on for the souls of men, and they have enlisted in God's army to fight evil at every hand. They are willing to give up homes, family, whatever it takes to serve God. They count the everlasting life more than the short life here; just as many killed.

"The second death": *The first death is only physical; the second is spiritual and eternal (20:14).*

Purpose": The purpose of Revelation is to reveal the person and the prophetic plan of Jesus Christ. Many events can be detected in this book.

- ❖ It is written to encourage believers to endure persecution and to persevere through suffering, knowing that the victory of Christ over the world and the Devil is assured and specific.
- ❖ The book was written to show how all prophecy focuses on Jesus Christ, His person, and His plan for the world.
- ❖ The book seeks to unite all the many areas of biblical prophecy, both Old and New Testaments, and to show how they congregate upon the second coming of Christ to rule the earth in His messianic kingdom. ❖ The book seeks to correct some moral and doctrinal problems that existed and still exist in the churches and instruct Christians in salvation, prophecy, the person of Christ, and Christian living.

❖ The book may attack the paganism and emperor worship of the Roman Empire, particularly against the emperor Domitian and his persecution of Christians. There are many possible hidden references to Rome's anti-Christian nature and activities in the book.

❖ Since it is predominantly prophetic, Revelation includes little historical material other than that. The seven churches addressed to whom the letters were current churches in Asia Minor modern Turkey. They were singled- out because John had ministered to them. Revelation is, first and foremost, a revelation about Jesus Christ (1:1).

❖ The book depicts Him as the risen, glorified Son of God ministering among the churches (1:10).

❖ "The faithful witness, the firstborn of the dead, and the ruler of the kings of the earth" (1:5).

❖ "The Alpha and the Omega" (1:8).

❖ The one "who is and who was and who is the come, the Almighty" (1:8).

CHAPTER 3

The Compromising Church

Revelation 2:12 "And to the angel of the church in Pergamos write.

These things saith he which hath the sharp sword with two edges sword. Pergamos: 313 to 590 A.D. - The State Church. Here we have the people who are in danger of doctrinal compromise. They are located about sixty miles north of Smyrna in Pergamos, which at one time was the official Asian center for the colonial cult. It was also the center of worship for four of the essential pagan cults of the day: Zeus, Athene, Dionysus, and Asclepius. Jesus, again, calls Himself by a different name. Here He is said to have "the sharp sword with the two edges." Of course, the sword with two edges is the Bible with the Old and New Testaments (Revelation 1:16).

They were not neglected. Jesus recognized their faithfulness despite the satanic environment in which they lived. In the original Greek, "hold fast" means "to hold onto anxiously with all of one's power."

These Christians were holding onto their faith with everything they had, and Jesus commended them for their faithfulness. According to Revelation 2:13, "I know thy works, and where thou dwellest, even where Satan's seat: and thou hold fast my name, and hast not denied my faith, even in those days wherein Antipas was my loyal believer, who was killed among you, where Satan dwelleth."

"Where Satan's seat": The headquarters of satanic hatred and a Gentile base for false religions. On the acropolis in Pergamum was a vast, throne-shaped altar to Zeus. In addition, Asclepius, the god of healing, was the god most associated with Pergamum. His snake-like form is still the medical symbol today. The famous medical school connected to his temple mingled medicine with misconception. One prescription called for the worshipper to sleep on the temple floor, allowing snakes to crawl over his body and infuse him with their healing power. Jesus not only knows their works; He knows everything about them. Judgment begins at the house of God because Jesus walks to and from checking them continually.

Jesus says that He knows where they dwell. He is referring to the very evil surroundings. It's an informative center. There were great libraries and places of worldly teaching.

In rebellion with God, this church is sinning, compromising with the heathen around them. Many times, worldly wisdom and faithfulness to God are not consistent. The Bible says that "The carnal mind is enmity against God" (Romans 8:7). Faith is not fact. The trained mind wants to prove by truths. Faith, I say again, is not fact:

According to Hebrews 11:1-2, *"Now faith is the substance of things hoped for, the evidence of things not seen." "For by it, the elders obtained a good report."*

Even though physically a few inches apart, the mind and heart are miles apart in the Spirit. As I have said before, there are many ways to view these. For our study, we will attempt to use the problems of this church to tell us what not to do in our church now.

God never changes. The things He resisted thousands of years ago are the things He fights today. God never changes; we change. If we are not careful, these changes will make us complacent about the sin in our life.

Jesus says that He knows where they dwell. He is referring to the very evil environments. It is a learning center. There were excellent archives and places of worldly teaching. Jesus knew this church in Pergamos would have a tough time. The evil in front of the church and the compromise in the church tries to draw more of these people out of the church. Maybe they had perfect plans, but they got horrible outcomes. Jesus goes so far as to call this evil city **"Satan's seat."** We know by this that evil reigned.

Jesus says to this church that you have my name on your church, and I am also aware you have not rejected me. Jesus even reminds them that He is mindful that Antipas was martyred because of his great faith in Jesus. This Satanic influence had come against Antipas and killed him. We must realize that we must not fellowship with those of nonbelief. We must witness and then go home.

Fellowshipping with the world brings compromise. The shame is that some of this has crept into this church as we see (Revelation 2:14).

Revelation 2:14 "But I have a few things against thee because thou hast there them that hold the doctrine of Balaam, who taught Balak to cast a stumbling block before the children of Israel, to eat things sacrificed unto idols, and to commit fornication." But the Lord also rebuked them for permitting members who practiced the "doctrine of Balaam and the Nicolaitans" to remain within their congregation.

"The doctrine of Balaam": Balaam tried disastrously to prostitute his prophetic gift and curse Israel for money offered him by Balak, king of Moab. So, he created a conspiracy to have Moabite women seduce Israelite men into intermarriage. The result was the unholy union of Israel with fornication and idolatrous feasts for the story of Balaam (Numbers chapters 22-25).

In his letter to Pergamos, Jesus assesses the conduct of some of these believers with the acts of the Israelites who compromised with the Moabites. He also condemned them for permitting the doctrine of the Nicolaitans to remain in their midst.

The word "Nicolaitan" arrives from two Greek words, one meaning "to conquer" and "the congregation." It is symbolic of developing a priestly order that ruled over the congregation according to Christ's command regarding serving one another (Matt. 23:8-9). The headship of Christ had been set aside in favor of a priestly order. The"things sacrificed unto idols" (Acts 15:19-29).

Revelation 2:15 "So hast thou also them that hold the doctrine of the Nicolaitans, which thing I hate.

- ❖ "Hast thou also": The teaching of the Nicolaitans led to the same conduct as Balaam's understandings.
- ❖ "Doctrine of the Nicolaitans" (Revelation verse 6).

The "doctrine of Balaam" was remarkably like the doctrine of the Nicolaitans. They tore down the true meaning of the spiritual gifts.

According to 2 Peter 2:1-2, "But there were false prophets among the people, even as there shall be false teachers among you, who privily shall bring in damnable heresies, even denying the Lord that bought them, and bring upon themselves swift destruction." "And many shall follow their pernicious ways; the way of truth shall be evil spoken of." Although they were victorious in keeping their faith during persecution, they opened the door to spiritual damage when they compromised with the world—apostasy and several religions, cults. Compromise is blending two ideas. The glossary says it is "to lay open to danger." Any compromised position opens you up to danger and immorality in spiritual matters.

Compromise is rampant throughout the Body of Christ. The Spirit of God calls us to allow the "sword of the Spirit," the Word of God, to uncover and remove negotiation just as a surgeon removes a cancerous growth. God cannot tolerate compromise! He hates it.

Even the slightest compromise opens the doors to further agreement, leading to even superior settlement and spiritual death. If you have compromised in any area of your life, you must do what Jesus told believers at Pergamos.

Revelation 2:16 "Repent; or else I will come unto thee quickly and fight against them with the sword of my mouth."

❖ "Sword of my mouth" (Rev. 1:16).

Repent means to be sorry and turn away from evil. Go in a new direction. Walk in the right, standing with the Lord. The sword that Jesus fights with is His Word. There is nothing more powerful than the Word of God. Jesus has not given up on them. He just wants them to change their ways.

Jesus issued a strict warning to the church at Pergamos: **"Repent; or else I will come unto thee quickly and fight against them with the sword of my mouth."**

Although the church's mainstream at Pergamos was not misled and did not follow the doctrine of the Balaamites and the Nicolaitans, they were guilty of disinterest toward the sin within their church.

But some slipped in, overlooked, and brought false teaching if you want to know more about all this false teaching (2 Peter 2).

Revelation 2:17 "He that hath an ear, let him hear what the Spirit saith unto the churches; To him that overcomes will I give to eat of the hidden manna, and will give him a white stone, and in the stone a new name written, which no man knows the saving he that received it."

As we said before, hear with our inner man. There is a battle, and we are God's soldiers. The Spirit and the flesh are locked in combat. When we allow the Spirit of God to control our flesh, then we are His. He is our God, and we are His people.

The stone, most think, was a diamond. It was probably the stone worn by the High Priest that had God's name. It was hidden from view next to the heart behind the Urim and the Thummim.

The other stones were symbolic of the Tribes of Israel, and all twelve of them were on the breastplate of the High Priest.

We have received the name of Jesus Christ if we are indeed His. We are Christians. I am happy to know that our name will be on it, whatever the stone is.

Jesus will feed us His hidden manna. Manna fell from heaven miraculously and fed the Israelites on their way to the Promised Land (Exodus 16:14-15). Just as Israel received manna, God promises to give the true believer the spiritual bread the unbelieving world cannot see Jesus Christ (John 6:51).

Whether this is spiritual or physical, I do not care. It will be all we need to maintain us. The original Ark of the Covenant, which the earthly Ark designed, has always been in heaven, hidden from earthly eyes.

The secrecy Jesus is revealing is Himself in His fullness.

- ❖ He is the Tree
- ❖ He is the Bread
- ❖ He is the Manna
- ❖ He is Life.

We, too, like Pergamos, must repent and come to Jesus with all that we are or ever hope to be. We are nothing until He fills us with his spirit.

- ❖ *"White stone":* When an athlete won in the games, he was often given, as part of his prize, a white stone which was an admission pass to the winner's celebration afterward. It may be an image of the moment when the overcomer will receive his ticket to the eternal victory celebration in heaven.
- ❖ *"New name":* A personal letter from Christ to the ones He loves, which serves as their admission to eternal glory. It is so unique that only the person who receives it will know what it is.
- ❖ Revelation 3:12 "The victorious one I will make a pillar in the temple of our God, and he will never again leave it. Upon him, I will write the name of our God and the name of the city of our God.
- ❖ The new Jerusalem that comes down out of heaven from our God and our new name".

According to some articles, I read: some huge churches will send their conservative congregations away in today's protestant denomination. They voted against same-sex marriage and non- celibate gay pastors. Their decision caused an uproar throughout the church; the congregations defied the ban on gay weddings, and many male and female pastors came out as homosexual they were ordinated.

Then they had observers of denominational politics, so they agreed to accept same-sex marriage and gay pastors. The people in the congregation that disagree may leave to form another denomination. In today's world, churches have compromised on homosexuality.

Leviticus 18:22 *"Thou shalt not lie with mankind, as with womankind: it is an abomination."*

By carnal knowledge of them, carnal copulation with them, and mixing bodies in like manner.

It is a sin commonly called sodomy, from the inhabitants of Sodom, greatly addicted to it, for which their city was destroyed by fire. By the apostle, those guilty of this sin are called "abusers of themselves with mankind" (1 Cor. 6:9).

"It is an abomination": it is a disgrace, horror, disgust, and outrage. It is so to God, as the above instance of his vengeance shows, and ought to be repugnant to men, as being not only contrary to the law of God but even contrary to nature itself. And what is never observed among brute creatures.

It is speaking of homosexual activities. **Homosexuality** is not only a sin; it is an abomination to God. The best way to explain this is with another Scripture. You shall not lie with a male as with a woman.

It is an abomination. Nor shall you mate with any animal to defile yourself with it. Nor shall any woman stand before an animal to mate with it. It is a perversion. (Lev. 18:22-23).

Romans 1:27 "And likewise also the men, leaving the natural use of the woman, burned in their lust one toward another; men with men working that which is unseemly, and receiving in themselves that recompense of their error which was meet."

Warning: in the following Scripture, how grave this sin is.

Romans 1:28 "And even as they did not like to retain God in their knowledge, God gave them over to a reprobate mind, to do those things which are not convenient;"

❖ *Reprobate* means rejected or worthless. It is a profoundly grave sin.

❖ Today, in many circles, the goodness and rightness of homosexuality are one of the most precise and authoritative moral convictions. It is one of the quickest and most moral revolutions in our history.

The church is warned about sin and exhorted to holiness. John's vivid pictures of worship in heaven both encourage and instruct believers. In a few other books of the Bible is, the ministry of angels so important. Revelation's primary theological contribution is to eschatology, i.e., the doctrine of last things. In Revelation, we learn about:

❖ The final political setup of the world.
❖ The previous battle of human history.
❖ The career and ultimate defeat of Antichrist.
❖ Christ's 1000-year earthly kingdom.
❖ The glories of heaven and the eternal state;
❖ The wicked and the righteous final form.

Ultimately, only Daniel rivals this book in declaring that God providentially rules over the kingdoms of men and will accomplish His sovereign purposes regardless of human or demonic opposition.

No other New Testament book presents more severe and complex instructive challenges than Revelation. The book's powerful explanations and astonishing interpretation have formed four main suggestive approaches:

Interprets Revelation as a description of first-century events in the Roman Empire. This view conflicts with the book's often repeated claim to be prophecy (1:3; 22:7, 10, 18, 19). It is impossible to see all the events in Revelation as already fulfilled. The second coming of Christ did not take place in the first century. Revelation is a complete view of church history from apostolic times to the present, seeing in the explanation such events as the philistine invasions of Rome, the rise of the Roman Catholic Church's popes, the advent of Islam, and the French Revolution.

This informative method robs Revelation of any meaning for those written. It also disregards the time restrictions the book itself places on the unfolding events (Rev. 11:2; 12:6, 14; 13:5). History has produced many different, often conflicting, understandings of the actual past events contained in Revelation. Revelation is a timeless understanding of the divine struggle between the forces of good and evil. In this view, the book contains neither ancient references nor prophetic prophecy. This view also ignores Revelations' prophetic character and separates the text from any organization with actual repeated events if carried to its reasonable decision. Revelation then becomes merely a set of tales intended to teach spiritual truth.

Insists that the events of (Rev.6-22) are yet future and that those chapters accurately and figuratively represent real people and events yet to appear on the world scene. It described the circumstances surrounding the second coming of Jesus Christ (Rev. 6-19), the Millennium and final judgment (Rev.20), and the eternal state (Rev. 21; 22).

Only this view does justice to Revelation's claim to be prophecy and interprets the book in the same basic-in-order style as (Rev. 1-3) and the rest of Scripture.

CHAPTER 4

The Corrupt Church

Revelation 2:18 "And unto the angel of the church in Thyatira writes, These things saith the Son of God, who hath his eyes like a flame of fire, and his feet are like fine brass.

According to the Bible:590 to 1517 A.D. - The Papal Church, the danger of moral compromise. The city of Thyatira was a vital commerce and trade center located about 40 miles southeast of Pergamos.

This church had been under Roman rule for nearly three centuries (ca. 190 B.C.). Since the city is in a long valley that swept 40 miles to Pergamum, it had no environmental protections and had a long history of being destroyed and rebuilt. Initially inhabited by soldiers of Alexander the Great, it was little more than a military establishment outpost to guard Pergamum.

This Thyatira is the same as where Lydia lived. In (Acts 16), we read:

Acts 16:14 "And a certain woman named Lydia, a seller of purple, of the city of Thyatira, which worshipped God, heard us: whose heart the Lord opened, that she concentrated unto the things which Paul spoke."

The church at Thyatira, many believe, is symbolic of the Roman Catholic Church and the period of that churches' eminence. I would not overemphasize that point.

- ❖ "Eyes like unto a flame of fire" (Rev.1:14).
- ❖ Jesus commended the church here at Thyatira for its good works.

Jesus shows this church His piercing "eyes," which can even discern the intents of the heart. His feet of "fine brass" show them that He truly is the final Judge (Rev. 19:15-29). Many Christians are not aware that they are worshiping idols. Some are so full of pride and self-deceit that their spiritual eyes blind them from seeing.

The areas of their lives where they have refused to let Jesus reign as Lord. Many believers today have made moral agreements. They no longer hold high standards of truthfulness. If you are guilty of moral compromise, or spiritual adultery, you must do what Jesus told these believers to do: Repent and then hold fast! Hold on to your truthfulness. Guard your Godly principles. Do not fall prey to moral compromise

We are looking at the spiritual and trying to see all the seven churches in our modern churches today, wherever possible, do not indicate fingers or call names. We must investigate ourselves before we start aiming our fingers.

- ❖ Speaking of idols, what could some of these be?
- ❖ Material possessions,
- ❖ Various lusts,
- ❖ Recreation,
- ❖ Entertainment,
- ❖ Career and selfish ambition.
- ❖ Dwell wisely as you think about the answer.

We are looking at the spiritual and trying to see all the seven churches in our modern churches today. Wherever possible, not aiming fingers or calling names. We must examine ourselves before we start seeking fingers. **The worship of the sun god** was rampant in this surrounding area, and perhaps, that is why we see Jesus offering the Morning Star to those who believe. Of course, Jesus is the Bright and Morning star (Rev. 28).

Revelation 2:19 "I know thy works, and charity, and service, and faith, and thy patience, and thy works; and the last to be more than the first."

Once again, Jesus sees beyond this outward display of good works and reveals a stronghold of Satan right during the church. The church of Pergamos was allowing a woman who called herself a prophetess to teach others that it was all right to mix pagan religions with Christianity. She was teaching and seducing people to commit fornication and compromise morally.

We are looking at the spiritual and trying to see all the seven churches in our modern churches today, wherever possible, not pointing fingers or calling names. We must examine ourselves before we start aiming our fingers.

This church here in Thyatira has great love and compassion and is a working church trying to improve the condition of the less fortunate around them. This church is patient, which is gained by many tribulations. It is not a stiff cold church, as some other churches are, but is a loving, caring church. It seems that the works of this church improve as they go along because the last are more than the first. It is a genuinely lovely statement that Jesus made about them.

Revelation 2:20 "Notwithstanding I have a few things against thee because thou suffer that woman Jezebel, who calleth herself a prophetess, to teach and seduce my servants to commit fornication, and eat things sacrificed unto idols."

All Through the Old Testament, this union of that which is holy with impure is considered by God as spiritual adultery. It was an abomination in His sight!

This false teacher is called "Jezebel," which may or may not have been her name but refers to her spirit. It references Jezebel in the Old Testament, who was the wife of King Ahab.

She was an idolatrous woman with underhanded methods to maintain her power. Jesus warned the church of Thyatira of coming judgment on this false teacher and all those who commit spiritual adultery by moral compromise. This "Jezebel" was given time to repent but refused (Rev. 2:21).

Now, those who her teaching had deceived were given a choice to repent or face severe judgment. In the Church today, most believers are not tempted to worship pagan idols of wood or stone, but they do worship other idols! It is one of the scriptures often used by certain denominations to say that women should not teach and preach.

If we carefully look at this, we will realize that **Jezebel** is not a woman, but a system of evil, whether taught by men or women. Fornication is the issue here, not that there is a woman in the church. Just as the Nicolaitans were not a country, Baal was a symbol of evil and not a specific place and person.

We need to look at fornication and see what it is. Fornication is incest or adultery of either sex indulging in unlawful lust. Everyone would agree that any minister of God who promoted these sins would be a **Jezebel** to Jesus.

Men and women who are believers in Christ are all the Bride of Christ. I do not believe that this **Jezebel** is all women who minister the Word of God, but just those who teach evil lust. In Galatians, we read that there is no male and female with God.

In Galatians 3:28, "There is neither Jew nor Greek, there is neither bond nor free, there is neither male nor female: for ye is all one in Christ Jesus.

"The same Paul that wrote for women to be silent in church (1 Corinthians 14:34) wrote this in Galatians. We also need to look at (Acts 2). According to the Bible: Acts 2:17-18, "And it shall come to pass in the last days, saith God, I will pour out of my Spirit upon all flesh: and your sons and your daughters shall prophesy, and your young men shall see visions, and your old men shall dream dreams:"

"And on my servants and my hand-maidens I will pour out in those days of my Spirit, and they shall prophesy:"

There is something we are not understanding, or else the Bible contradicts itself. We know the Bible does not contradict itself. We must look more carefully at what the Scriptures mean. The error comes in wrong messages that some women or men bring. The Jezebel here could be a woman, but if she is, it is not that she is a sinful woman; it is an evil letter that is wrong. Let us look at one more Scripture in Acts.

According to the Bible: Acts 21:8-9, "And the next day we that were of Paul's company left and came unto Caesarea: and we entered into the house of Philip the evangelist, which was one of the seven; and abode with him." "And the same man had four daughters, virgins, which did prophesy." There are many examples just like this of Philip's daughters. We must all be careful about condemning others in their ministry. Look carefully at the context it is written in before speaking out against others. Jezebel calls herself a prophetess. It appears that whoever this is or whatever group this represents, they promote feelings of the flesh, not the Spirit.

We are warned not to eat things sacrificed to idols throughout the Bible knowingly. *Revelation 2:21 "And I gave her space to repent of her fornication, and she repented not."*

We must carefully look at what must be repented. The sin here is fornication. She was not to repent of preaching but repent of fornication.

In the days that John wrote this, there were evil churches that even had harlots working in the church for the members' convenience.

In our time, **the satanic churches promote sex**. Some churches teach that homosexuality and lesbianism are alternate lifestyles. My Bible says they are an abomination to God (Leviticus 18:22). You can easily see this church spiritually in Thyatira in these churches. Not only did Thyatira need to repent, but modern churches that teach this abomination.

Revelation 2:22 "Behold, I will cast her into a bed, and them that commit adultery with her into great tribulation, except they repent of their deeds."

"Cast her into a bed": "bed." Having given this woman time to repent, God was to judge her upon a bed. Since she used a luxurious bed to commit her immorality and the reclining couch at the idol feast to eat things offered to false gods, He was to give her a bed in hell where she would lie forever. It could be both physical and spiritual adultery.

The people who get involved in these sex sins are guilty. It is no excuse to sin because your minister tells you that you are not guilty. Try every message you hear by what the Bible teaches. Do not be deceived by any false prophet, male or female. Their repentance is of their deeds, not whether they were male or female. You are only responsible for your sins, not what others have said or done to you.

Revelation 2:23 "And I will kill her children with death; and all the churches shall know that I am he which search the reins and hearts: and I will give unto every one of you according to your works."

"Her children": The church was about 40 years old as John wrote, and her teaching had produced a second generation, encouraging the same immorality. The reins word *means "the innermost mind," perhaps the unconscious mind.* The heart will be judged. The motive behind our deeds is just as important as the deed. God has perfect, intimate knowledge of every human nature; no evil can be hidden from Him (Psalm 7:9; Prov. 24:12; Jer. 11:20; 17:10; 20:12).

In the Scripture above, God will not always overlook sin in the church. When His judgment falls, it will begin in the church. Punishment will be swift and so severe that other churches will look and tremble at the sentence. The work spoken of here is the heart and mind works that come to maturity in actual deeds. Good or evil begins in the mind and heart. Beautiful words cannot come from a bad heart, but beautiful acts cannot either. What we are inside will show in what we do for God.

"According to your works": Always the basis for future judgment (Rev. 20:12-13; Matt. 16:27; Rom. 2:6). Deeds or works do not save (Eph. 2:8-9), but they evidence salvation (James 2:14-26).

Revelation 2:24 "But unto you I say, and unto the rest in Thyatira, as many as have not this doctrine, and which have not known the depths of Satan, as they speak; I will put upon you none other burdens."

"The depths of Satan": This unbelievable libertinism and license was the fruit of pre-gnostic teaching that one was free to engage and investigate the realm of Satan and participate in evil with the body without damaging the spirit (1 John).

What principle is spoken of here? The direction of fleshly lust and fornication. The code says you can do what you please if you are baptized. Jesus wants a virtuous virgin for a bride. Jesus wants us to be holy as He is holy. Sin must not be practiced if we are Christians.

Jesus will forgive us of our sins if we ask Him, but we must not go back into that sin repeatedly. Our heart must desire to live above sin.

Revelation 2:25 "But that which ye have already hold fast till I come."
Warning: here also, that even though this church speaks of promoting sin, an individual can repent and be saved even in this situation. God does not judge groups. Jesus judges us for our sin.

It would be a terrible burden to have no other church to go to than one that taught fornication. He tells them to hold fast to sound doctrine until He comes.

Revelation 2:26 "And he that overcomes, and keep my works unto the end, to him will I give power over the nations: "overcome" (verse 7).

Here, you see that Jesus stipulates His works are what is to be done. It also means that we should not just do a little and get self-pleased but stay with the Lord's work to the very end. Just as Jesus told the parable of the good servant (Luke 19), we must be a good servants and bring the fruits of our labor to Jesus. Jesus says the servant (Luke 19:17) was to rule over ten cities. He also promises that his faithful will lead. Remember, the power is Jesus'. He gives us our strength. This power is to do His will as we govern. We are working under Jesus' direction. He is our leader.

Revelation 2:27 "And he shall rule them with a rod of iron; as the vessels of a potter shall they be broken to shivers: even as I received of my Father."

❖ **The "rod of iron"** means the rule will be strict and unbending.

Accurately "shepherds them with an iron rod." During the millennial kingdom, Christ will enforce His will and protect His sheep with His iron scepter from any who would seek to harm them (Psalm 2:9).

The rule will be like a shepherd leads if they follow Jesus, but if not, they shall be broken to pieces. This rod spoken of could be a shepherd's or a king's. The rod of correction will be used in love. Jesus was given all power on earth, under the world, and in heaven by the Father.

❖ **"Shivers" means pieces.**

Revelation 2:28 "And I will give him the morning star."

Jesus is the Bright and Morning Star. He promises to give Himself to those who will follow Him. Although the morning star has already dawned in our hearts (2 Peter 19), we will have Him in His fullness someday.

Revelation 2:29 "He that hath an ear, let him hear what the Spirit saith unto the churches."

Warning: again, this letter is not just given to this one church of Thyatira, but churches, plural. We must take heed to the signs. Open the ears of our hearts and receive Jesus in His fullness.

CHAPTER 5

The Dead Church

Revelation Chapter 3

In Revelation chapter 3, we continued with the last three of the seven churches. Revelation 3:1 "And unto the angel of the church in Sardis write, These things saith he that hath the seven Spirits of God, and the seven stars; I know thy works, that thou hast a name that thou lives, and art dead."

Sardis: The Danger of Spiritual Death. 1517 to1790 A.D., the Modernized church. This church at Sardi's is seen by many as the reformation church. In this study, we will look at this church in the light of our modern churches.

Sardis is located 35 miles southeast of *Thyatira*. It was the capital of Lydia and was once a portrait of strength, fertility, and wealth. Idolatry and immorality were its reputations.

The church at Sardi's had "a name," a good reputation, and it appeared to be alive. But there was nothing but inward deadness.

Their deadness was partially due to some defilement because the Word says there were only "a few" that had not been defiled (Rev. 3:4).

These people desperately needed the ministry of the Holy Spirit. The mention of the "seven Spirits of God" is a character reference to the sevenfold ministry of the Spirit found in Isaiah:

Isaiah 11:2 "And the spirit of the Lord shall rest upon him, the spirit of wisdom and understanding, the spirit of counsel and might, the spirit of knowledge and the fear of the Lord."

This church needed the ministry of the Holy Spirit in all areas. If you are spiritually dead, you need these ministries also:

- ❖ *The Spirit of Wisdom:* A lifeless dying church or individual needs to seek the wisdom of God. (Isaiah 11: 2).
- ❖ *The Spirit of Understanding:* A lifeless dying church or individual needs a proper understanding of their condition so they can correct it. (Isaiah 11: 2)
- ❖ *The Spirit of Counsel:* A lifeless dying church or individual needs to heed the counsel of God. (Isaiah 11: 2)
- ❖ *The Spirit of Might:* A lifeless dying church or individual needs new strength to enter its dead body. (Isaiah 11: 2)
- ❖ *The Spirit of Knowledge*: A lifeless dying church or individual needs to flow in renewed revelation knowledge. (Isaiah 11: 2)
- ❖ *The Spirit of Fear of the Lord:* A lifeless dying church or individual needs to have their fear of the Lord revived. (Isaiah 11: 2).

If you feel spiritually dead or your church is dying corporately, then you must follow the five-fold plan that the Spirit gave to the church at Sardis (Rev. 3:3):

- ❖ *Be Watchful:* To "Rouse yourself and keep awake." It is time for us to wake up, become alert to the signs of the time, and be active for God as never before.
- ❖ *Strengthen:* Take hold of the things that remain and are ready to die in your life and strengthen them through prayer and the Word. It is not your strength. It is God's strength.
- ❖ *Remember:* Reflect on the promises of God, what you have received and heard in times past.
- ❖ *Hold Fast:* Hold fast to your faith and God's Word.
- ❖ *Repent:* Repent so you will be ready for the return of Christ and not caught unaware.

This church is evident to me. When some congregation members went to a specific church, these churches were outwardly influential in the Lord. People shouted and said amen—people praying for the sick. Then suddenly, there were physical changes in the services time and bible study and prayer. God's plan from the beginning has been for the churches to be one in Spirit. You cannot endorse Christianity.

A church had a Sunday service at three am. People began to know something was wrong. The Shepherd had affairs with one of the ministers, and she got pregnant with his child while he was still married.

It brought about a great division, and some members stayed in the church while others followed his wife out of the church. What had been a way of life for many for the church in their lives had changed. Some people just returned from oversea and got a station close to their hometown. The shouting stopped; the church became too formal for the amen corner. The first thing they knew, they found themselves in a cold and divided church, not the warm, caring church they had loved so well. The church never dared run over fifteen minutes; we had to stay on schedule. Bible studies became less and scarcer. No prayer either.

The congregation was unaware of how essential Bible reading and study were at home. Their church, which loved all Christian people, had made a diversion.

They believe that churches like this are what the Sardis church is all about. They started simply fantastic, but as time went on, they faded away.

Warning: Jesus speaks of the seven Spirits of God. When the gifts of the Holy Spirit are denied and even spoken evil of, the true church will dry up. The power of God is in His Spirit. Therefore, Jesus said to this church this.

The Spirit has gone: This church is still teaching and preaching *Christianity but denying the power.* Many use this scripture in 2 Timothy a lot, but it perfectly describes the time we live and describes this church at Sardis best of all.

> ❖ *2 Timothy 3:1 "This also know, that in the last days perilous times shall come."*
> ❖ *2 Timothy 3:5 "Having a form of godliness but denying the power thereof: from such turn away."*

Several churches would have us believe the gifts of the Spirit are not in operation today. If they are not, it is because of our lack of faith. God never changes; we change.

A man without a spirit is like a horse who has lost his gust. A church without the Spirit is slowly dying; there is no prayer.

God does not want us to reasonably go to church because it is expected of us once a week. He wants us to look forward to fellowshipping with Him. The love in our hearts for Jesus should make us desire to go to church and receive everything He has for us.

Revelation 3:2: "Be watchful, and strengthen the things that remain, ready to die: for I have not found thy works perfect before God."

Jesus tells them here; there is still some good in this church; build upon those things. Even the interest in this church is being watered down to the point that even it is about to die. I believe the works here spoken of are not saying they are not doing jobs, but that their results are biased more toward the world than toward God.

This church is very social-minded and helps local government with their projects, if I understand it.

If you counted how many actual transformations were made within the last year, you would be amazed at the shortage, and they do not return to the church. What we call good works and what God calls good works are two entirely different things. God looks at the Spirit, and we look at the physical.

Revelation 3:3 "Remember how thou hast received and heard, and hold fast, and repent. If thou shalt not watch, I will come on thee as a thief, and thou shalt not know what hour I will come upon thee."

"Come on thee as a thief": Here, the reference is not Christ's second coming (16:15; 1 Thess. 5:2; 2 Peter 3:10), but to His sudden and unexpected coming to His unrepentant, dead church to inflict harm and destruction.

Here again, Jesus is saying, your message at the beginning was alright; go back to that, the pure Word of God. Some new Bible translations are watering Jesus down to the point that He is not God in them.

Some Bible colleges would have their people believe that: Jesus was not born of a virgin, that the Red Sea did not part, that a large fish did not indeed swallow Jonah and many more things.

You see, they are reducing the wondrous workings of God and trying to appraise them with what they call practical knowledge. It is just another attack of Satan to destroy the majesty of Christianity. These are basic to belief in salvation through Jesus Christ.

If a mere man died for your sins, you are lost. Jesus was God manifest in the flesh. He was the perfect Lamb of God. He was and is Life. To deny that He was born of a virgin denies that He is God the Son. You see, His Father is God.

These false teachers say the Red Sea did not part but was just a swampy area. If this is true, explain how the Egyptian soldiers drowned. You see, the whole thing is a plot to deny the divinity of Christ. It is exceptionally hazardous. If we deny Him, He will deny us before the Father (Matthew 10:33).
However, these false teachings include teaching that there is no heaven and no hell. That they are just a state of mind. The Bible speaks clearly

about both and even tells us what they will be like. All of this is somewhat ridiculous.

We must believe the Bible in its totality or not believe it. As for me, I think it in its entirety. Jesus was Immanuel, God with us. **In denying Jesus as the Christ, the Son of the Living God is to deny salvation through Him."**

Revelation 3:4 "Thou hast a few names even in Sardis which have not defiled their garments, and they shall walk with me in white: for they are worthy."

"In white": All the redeemed white garments (compare 6:11; 7:9, 13; 19:8, 14) speak of holiness and purity. Such white robes are reserved for Christ (Matt. 17:2; Mark 9:3), holy angels (Matt. 28:3; Mark 16:5), and the glorified church (19:8, 14). White robes were worn at festivals and celebrations in the earliest world.

Jesus says here there are a few people even in this church of Sardis, or we have fallen away from church now that is still strong in the Lord. They believe in the truth rather than a lie.

A dirty garment is one not washed in the blood of the Lamb. You see, the white that we must wear is a white robe made whiter than snow by being washed in the blood of the Lamb.

It is our robe of righteousness that we will wear in heaven. *"Righteousness" means right standing with God.*

Most of the churches now that are like this church in Sardis do not like to preach or teach on the blood of Jesus. It was the shed blood that defeated Satan and purchased our salvation. We read in Hebrews; just how vital this shed blood is.

Hebrews 9:22 "And almost all things are by the law purged with blood, and without shedding of blood is no remission."

If we are not washed in the blood of the Lamb, then we are walking in sin. In chapter seven of Revelation, we can study the lesson about the significant number from all nations standing around the throne in their white robes.

Revelation 7:14 "And I said unto him, Sir, thou know. And he said to me, these are they which came out of great tribulation, washed their robes, and made them white in the blood of the Lamb."

To deny the power of the blood would deny us our right to stand before the throne of God. Do not be deceived. Believe the Word of God, the Bible. Let no one convince you that it is not valid.

Revelation 3:5 "He that overcomes, the same shall be clothed in white raiment; and I will not blot out his name out of the book of life, but I will confess his name before my Father, and before his angels."

"See Book of Life": A divine journal records all those whom God has chosen to save and who, therefore, are to possess eternal life (13:8; 17:8; 20:12, 15; 21:27; 22:19; Dan. 12:1; Luke 10:20). In some cases, He will erase your names from the book of life, as city officials often did of undesirable people on their rolls. It is one of the most significant assurances in the Bible. We must overcome the world and its teachings to inherit eternal life. If we do overcome, our name is written in the Lamb's Book of Life, ensuring eternal life in heaven with Jesus.

If we confess Jesus before men, He will confess us before His Father. Jesus is the Judge. We stand or fall by His command.

You see from the statement above that overcoming is not a bed of roses but a battle. Jesus won the war. We must enlist in this army of Jesus. We must fight to the death, if necessary, for the standards, He has taught us in the Bible.

Be strong; do not be led away by all these new teachings of heaven on earth before Jesus comes. The only time the world will be like heaven is the 1000-year reign of Jesus here (Rev.20). Withstand the devil, and he will flee from you. Be part of the elect who cannot be deceived.

Revelation 3:6 "He that hath an ear, let him hear what the Spirit saith unto the churches." Again, we are told to hear what the Spirit said to the churches.

CHAPTER 6

The Faithful Church

Revelation 3:7 "And to the angel of the church in Philadelphia write; These things saith he that is holy, he that is true, he that has the key of David, that opens, and no man shuts, and shuts, and no man opens;" I know your works, see, I have set before you an open door, and no one can shut it; for you have a little strength, have kept my word, and have not denied my name.

It is the **church in Philadelphia.** Everyone wants to be like the church of Philadelphia. This church is thought to be a missionary church. If we carefully look at this church, we can suppose we will be able to see a church in our present time. The church would be strong and active in the gifts of the Spirit. They would be teaching holiness and righteousness. The people would not be tolerant of compromising. They would not be just any specific denomination but trained in Jesus and led by the Holy Spirit of God. This church would be nurturing the Holy Spirit rather than bringing the world into the church.

Philadelphia: The Danger of Failing to Advance (1790 to 1900 A.D.). The Missionary Church.

The city of Philadelphia was 25 miles southeast of Sardis on an 800-foot rise. To this church, which Christ says has a little strength, the Lord comes to open an opportunity of chance that no force in hell can shut. "Possessing the key of David" means that He has the authority to extend this supernatural door. The reference to those who "say they are Jews and are not" describes all who reject Jesus Christ. Romans 2 clarifies what constitutes a Jew.

Romans 2:28-29 "For he is not a Jew, which is one outwardly; neither is that circumcision, which is outward in the flesh:" "But he is a

Jew, which is one inwardly; and circumcision is that of the heart, in the spirit, and not in the letter; whose praise is not of men, but of God."

Jesus shows Himself to this church of Philadelphia in the very same way that they worship Him.

- ❖ **He is Holy.**
- ❖ **Jesus tells us to "be Holy even as He is Holy" (Lev. 11:44, 1 Peter 1:15).**
- ❖ **He shows Himself as truth.**
- ❖ **He is "the Way, The Truth, and the Life" (John 14:6).**

Jesus is the one that opens the door to heaven or hell for us. Jesus is the door to heaven. He is the only one who can shut or open either door. He took the keys of suffering away from the devil when Jesus went there and preached. Jesus is the final Judge for everyone's resting place.

This church in Philadelphia and its symbolic church in the present day are not only well informed of who Jesus is, but they are imitating their lives after His. They are the very chosen. It is full of the Word, so complete that it would be difficult to deceive them.

God promises these believers that He will keep them from the hour of temptation that will come upon the world.

- ❖ Is "the hour"?
- ❖ Is it a period of trial?
- ❖ Future from the time of John's writing.
- ❖ To be worldwide.
- ❖ The promise to "keep thee out of" the hour.

These details clarify that the event describes the Great Tribulation (in Mat. 24:15-22). These believers at Philadelphia, who have only a "little strength," have kept God's Word and have not denied His Name. God promises that they will become pillars in the temple of God (Rev.

3:12). This church may have been small or inconsiderable sources, but God was going to make them strong. They are promised an open door. In Scripture, an open door refers to Christ (John 10:7), an opening to preach the Gospel (Acts 5:19-20), and the rapture of the Church (Rev. 4:1).

Each of these may be translated as the "open door" promised to this church, even as each can be applied to the Church today. In these end times, God is opening many immense doors of the chance that there is always an inherent danger of failing to proceed at Christ's command. You may feel you have only a little strength, but God can make you a solid and mighty pillar in His Kingdom, a spiritual warrior who can walk through every door He opens. What is holding you back from fulfilling God's call for your life?

- ❖ Fear
- ❖ Your finances
- ❖ Your health
- ❖ Your relationships with others
- ❖ The World
- ❖ Pride
- ❖ Family
- ❖ People

God has set before you an open door that no man can shut. All the demons in hell cannot close it. Jesus is the way. All you must do is walk through those entrances in the almighty power of God.

Revelation 3:8 "I know thy works: behold, I have set before thee an open door, and no man can shut it: for thou hast a little strength, and hast kept my word, and hast not denied my name."

Jesus is aware of everything the churches are doing. He has first-hand knowledge because He walks in the church. Jesus is the door and has offered Himself for us to go through to heaven. The

door that Jesus opens can only be closed by Him. Jesus cares for His own.

It is inspiring here that He says this church has a little strength. It is true of all firm believers. In our weakness, Jesus is strong. The power that nourishes us and sees us through is His, not our own. The perfect statement Jesus makes about this church is that they have kept His Word.

We, too, must be careful to represent the Word of God. The Bible is our training book for living. If we change it in any way, the guidelines will not work. But many have watered down the Word until it has been no effect and lost power. We must not interfere with the regime. This church started here might be small, but big in love and the Holy Spirit. Again, we see so many rejecting the name of Jesus. I believe here that the character they are leaving is that Jesus was God. We touched on it before, but it is worth saying again. Today, most churches want to call Jesus: Prophet, Teacher, Healer, or Man. Very few realize that He was God visible in the flesh (God the Son). It is a vital thing and will be stated more as we read the word of God.

Revelation 3:9 "Behold, I will make them of the synagogue of Satan, which say they are Jews, and are not, but do lie; behold, I will make them come and worship before thy feet and know that I have loved thee."

There is no change in someone who follows Satan and someone who pretends to be a Christian and is not. Both are lost.

The "synagogue of Satan" is just a place of worship where God is not Lord. A Jewish synagogue could be of Satan if evil reigned. A body of Christians meeting could also be a synagogue of Satan if the accurate Word of God is not taught and received.

There will come a time when the Truth will be victorious. The church, which does not compromise and exists unto the end, shall reign with Christ. Jesus is just encouraging this church that has tried so hard that there will be a rewarding day. The Christians will rule over those who have rejected Jesus for 1000 years here on this earth. Jesus loves the faithful. He has His ear turned to our needs.

Revelation 3:10 "Because thou hast kept the word of my patience, I will keep thee from the hour of temptation, which shall come upon all the world, to try them that dwell upon the earth."

A promise that Christ will rapture true believers out of the world before the Tribulation period begins. The "hour of temptation" is the period of worldwide testing that has not yet occurred (Dan. 12:1; Matt. 24:21, 29).

Christ promises to keep them from the period of the Tribulation. That is, they will not even join this period of history. The Tribulation is to try or judge "them that dwell upon the earth," those who are connected to the earth and its governmental system. Believers are not even included in this term (Phil. 3:18-20; 1 Peter 2:11; Rev. 6:10; 11:10; 13:8, 12, 14; 17:8).

Now trials, tribulations, and temptations come to all. The group has been tested and found to stand in their temptation. There is a time of testing and a time of victory or defeat. Jesus was enticed for forty days and nights and came out victorious.

When trials come, we can do one of two things. We can stand against the temptation and experience victory, or take the easy way out and succumb to temptation and fall to defeat. If you are a Christian and if the temptation wins, you will go through this temptation repeatedly until you stand against it and overcome it.

This group revealed here has stood against these enticements, so their promise from Jesus is that they will not be required to go through the great temptation. There is a time needed of God when the temptations, tribulations, and trials will be so great that it will be next to impossible to stand. An hour with God can be any particular time.

God's time and our time are not identical. This hour revealed here definitely does not mean sixty minutes, but the Tribulation period.

There will be seven years of tribulation at the end of the Gentile age. The last three and a half years of this will be the wrath of God. God has promised the believers in the Lord Jesus Christ that we will be saved from the wrath to come.

We think this is the case here. The temptation here, we believe, is the same as the tribulation. (Revelation 7:9 and 7:13-14), warns of the Christians who are saved from the agonizing temptation at the end of three and a half years of tribulation.

Revelation 7:9 *"After this I beheld, and, lo, a great multitude, which no man could number, of all nations, and kindreds, and people, and tongues, stood before the throne, and before the Lamb, clothed with white robes, and palms in their hands;."*

Revelation 7:13-14 *"And one of the elders answered, saying unto me, what are these arrayed in white robes? And whence came they?" "And I said unto him, Sir, thou know. And he said to me, these are they which came out of great tribulation, washed their robes, and made them white in the blood of the Lamb."*

We see these are disciples in Jesus the Christ the saved, who have been brought out held in great tribulation.

❖ **Matthew 24** describes the severity of this great tribulation.

Matthew 24:21-22 "For then shall be great tribulation, such as was not since the beginning of the world to this time, no, nor ever shall be." "And except those days should be shortened, no flesh should be saved: but those days shall be shortened for the elect's sake."

The age of temptation this Scripture (Revelation 3:10) is speaking about. The believers in Jesus will be taken out just before the temptation becomes impossible to withstand. So many people believe the believers will not be tried; I think they will be tested to prove whether their belief is genuine or insignificant. They will not be pushed further than what they can endure.

"I Come quickly": The time of the deliverance mentioned is here identified with the return of Christ to His church (the Rapture). The "temple" may relate either to the millennial kingdom or New Jerusalem. The genuine believer will be given a place of service and honor before God. The threefold reference to the "name" guarantees eternal security in Christ. The "name of my God" shows ownership. The *name of the city" indicates heavenly citizenship*. And "my new name," co-heirship with Christ.

Revelation 3:11 "Behold, I come quickly: hold that fast which thou hast, that no man takes thy crown."

"I come quickly": This is not the hostile earthly judgment described (3; 2:5, 16), nor the final decision (Rev.19); it is a hopeful event. Christ will return to take His church out of the hour of the trail (2 Thess. 2:1).

This statement is just verifying what we said above that there is a test time for the believers. We will be required to stand; when we do, we will be raptured and saved from the horrors.

Revelation 3:12 "Him that overcometh will I make a pillar in the temple of my God, and he shall go no more out: and I will write upon him the name of my God, and the name of the city of my God, which is new Jerusalem, which cometh down out of heaven from my God: and [I will write upon him] my new name."

Again, we see here that there is something that we must overcome. A person many times is spoken of as a pillar of the community or a pillar of the church, which just means that they are strong and are holding up the church. These people would be like founding fathers, high in principles. They would be the ones who would see to it that the church stays on solid ground.

This writing of the name of God just means that we are sealed into His kingdom. If we were to read very much about this city, we would find that sometimes it is spoken of as a bride. The believers in Jesus are the bride of Christ. The city's name is on the believers, indicating that we are the bride of Christ.

This new name of Jesus written upon us shows that we are Jesus' possession. We are His; we have been bought and paid for with His blood. When it says we shall no longer go out, it means that our eternal home is here with Jesus.

However, (Verse 12) says that we, the believers, have put our trust and faith in Jesus and endured hardship. We then have an eternity of nothing but pure joy in this New Jerusalem with Jesus. Once we have passed from death into life through accepting Jesus as our Lord and Savior, we are sealed by Jesus Himself. We belong to Him. No one can snatch us back away from Him. Jesus has the keys. Look to Him and no other. He is salvation.

Revelation 3:13 "He hath an ear, let him hear what the Spirit saith unto the churches."

Once again, we are told to hear what the Spirit said to the churches by Jesus Himself, who spoke these words like all these messages to these churches are printed in red. He reminds us once again to open the ears of our understanding of His teachings.

Traveling 45 miles southeast of Philadelphia, one would arrive at the fortified city of Laodicea, where several significant roads converge. Medicine, production of eye ointment, wool distribution, manufacturing, and banking brought fame to this city. It is interesting to note how Christ related His message to these qualities of the city (verses 17-18). The people of Laodicea felt they needed nothing. They boasted of their riches, yet they were spiritually poor. Although they were famous for their eye salve, they were spiritually blind. They were known for their fine wool, but they were spiritually naked. How do you do if you are lukewarm?

Ask yourself these questions:

❖ Are you committed to evangelism and missions?
❖ Are you committed to living a holy life?
❖ Are you committed to your local church fellowship?
❖ Are you committed to spending time in prayer, worship, and the Word?
❖ Are you committed to other believers in the Body of Christ?
❖ Are you actively supporting God's work with your finances?

CHAPTER 7

The Lukewarm Church

The people at Laodicea were spiritually lukewarm, and Christ said their condition must be remedied. He commanded them to do three things which we also must do if we want to eradicate our Lukewarmness:

- ❖ *"Buy of me Gold, Tried in the Fire."* The fire refines gold. Let the Word of God refine you spiritually and burn away the Lukewarmness in your life. The words of the Lord are pure: as silver tried in a furnace of earth, purified seven times (Psalms 12:6).
- ❖ Buy of me White Raiment". Allow God to change you by making a renewed commitment to righteous living. Eph. 4:24 "And that ye put on the new man, which after God is created in righteousness and true holiness."
- ❖ **"Anoint your Eyes so You Can See."** Receive the decisive revelation of God through Jesus Christ, which will open your blinded eyes and effect actual change in your life.
- ❖ "For God, who commanded the light to shine out of darkness, hath shined in our hearts, to give the light of the knowledge of the glory of God in the face of Jesus Christ." (2 Cor. 4:6).

The book of Colossians and this message here was to the Laodiceans (Colossians 4:13; 16). They were a very prominent area. It seems that Paul and Jesus in the book of Revelation warned them about their lack of zeal in their church.

When Scripture declares that Jesus is the "Amen," it means that He is the divine "Yes" to the prayers of God's people whenever they are made in accord with God's will.

2 Cor. 1:20 "For all the promises of God in him are yea, and in him Amen, unto the glory of God by us."

- ❖ *Jesus is spoken of as "faithful." He is worthy of our faith in Him.*
- ❖ **Jesus is Truth**, faithful because He experienced it. It does not waver. It is a fact. He created everything on the earth as we know it. We can easily see from John that Jesus made everything.

According to John 1:1-3, "In the beginning was the Word, the Word was with God, and the Word was God." "The same was at the beginning with God." "He made all things, and without him was not anything made."

Jesus is the Creator of all things.

- ❖ Sardis--the ancient capital of Lydia, the kingdom of wealthy Croesus, on the river Pactolus. The address to this Church is full of rebuke. It does not seem to have been in vain, for the Bishop of Sardis in the second century was eminent for piety and learning.
- ❖ He visited Palestine to assure himself and his flock of the Old Testament canon and wrote an epistle on the subject (Apostolic History, 4.26).
- ❖ He also wrote a commentary on the Apocalypse (Religious History, 4.26).
- ❖ He that hath the seven Spirits of God--that is, He who hath all the fulness of the Spirit (Re 1:4; 4:5; 5:6,)
- ❖ with which compare Zec 3:9; 4:10, demonstrating The Godhead). This attribute implies His infinite power by the Spirit to convict of sin and a hollow profession.

According to the Bible, the seven stars-- (Re 1:16, 20). Therefore, his having the seven stars, or presiding ministers, flows from His having the seven Spirits, or the fulness of the Holy Spirit. The human ministry is the fruit of Christ's sending down the gifts of the Spirit. Stars imply brilliancy and glory; the fulness of the Spirit, and the usefulness of brilliant light in Him, form a designed contrast to the formality which He reproves. These names lives, deceased-- (1Ti 5:6; 2Ti 3:5; Tit 1:16; Eph 2:1, 5; 5:14).

"A name," that is, a reputation. Sardis was famed among the churches for spiritual vitality; yet the Heart-searcher, who sees not as man sees, pronounces her dead; how excellent examining of heart should her case create among even the best of us! Laodicea deceived herself as to her actual state (Re 3:17), but it is not written that she had a high name among the other churches, as Sardis had. Be--Greek. "Become," what thou art not, "watchful," or "wakeful," literally, "waking." Therefore, these things which remain: Strengthen those thy remaining few graces, which, in thy deadly spiritual slumber, are not yet entirely extinct. "The things that remain" can hardly mean "the person who is not yet dead but ready to die." Re 3:4 implies that the "few" faithful ones at Sardi's were not "ready to die" but were full of life. The two oldest manuscripts read, "we're ready," literally, "were about to die," namely, at the time when you "reinforce" them.

It implies that "thou art dead," Re 3:1, is to be taken with restraint, for those must-haves some life that reinforces the remaining things. Perfect-accurately, "filled up in full balance"; Translate, "complete." Weighed in the stability of Him who requires living faith as the motive of works and found wanting. Before God--Greek, "in the sight of God." Christ's judgment is God the Father's judgment. In the sight of men, Sardis had "a name of living": "so many and so great are the responsibilities of pastors, that he or she who would, in reality, fulfill even a third of them, would be revered holy by men, whereas, if content with that alone, he would be sure not to escape hell."

Note: in Sardis and Laodicea alone of the seven, we read of no conflict with foes within or without the Church.

Not that either had renounced the appearance of resistance to the world, but neither had the faithfulness to witness for God by word and example, to "torment them that dwelt on the earth" (Re 11:10).

How thou hast received-- (Col 2:6; 1Th 4:1; 1Ti 6:20). **What Sardis is to "remember"** is not how joyfully she had received the Gospel message originally. Still, how the precious deposit was committed to her originally, so she could not say she had not "received and heard" it. The Greek is not aorist (as in Re 2:4, as to Ephesus, "Thou didst leave thy first love"), but "thou hast received" (perfect), and still hast the permanent deposit of doctrine committed to thee. The word "keeps" ("hold fast") expands and treaties with this sense. "Keep" or observe the commandment you have received and didst hear. Therefore, they heard--Greek aorist, "didst hear," namely when the Gospel doctrine was committed to thee. Trench explains "how," with what presentation of the Spirit and power from Christ's ambassadors the truth came to you, and how thoroughly and passionately you first received it.

Similarly, "Regard to her former character (how it once stood) ought to guard Sardis against the future hour, whatsoever it shall be, proving fatal to her." But it is not likely that the Spirit repeats the same exhortation virtually to Sardis as to Ephesus. If therefore--seeing thou art so warned, if, nevertheless, come on thee as a thief in exceptional judgment as a Church, with the same stealthy and surprisingly as shall be my visible second coming. The thief gives no notice of his approach. Christ applies the language that describes His second coming in its most total sense to tell His coming in extraordinary judgments on churches and states such as Jerusalem (Mt 24:4-28). These particular judgments being preventative earnests of that tremendous last coming. "The last day is hidden from us that we may observe every day. Twice Christ in the days of His flesh spoke the exact words (Mt 24:42, 43; Lu 12:39, 40); and so sincerely had His words engraved on the minds of the apostles that they are often repeated in their writings (Re 16:15; 1Th 5:2, 4, 6; 2Pe 3:10).

The Greek proverb was that "the feet of the avenging deities are shod with wool," expressing the noiseless approach of the divine judgments and their possible nearness now when they were. The three oldest manuscripts prefix "but" or "nevertheless" despite thy spiritual deadness and omit "even." The names--persons named in the book of life (Re 3:5) known by name by the Lord as His own. These had the reality corresponding to their name, not a mere name among men as living while dead (Re 3:1). The gracious Lord does not overlook any exceptional cases of real saints during unreal professors. Some may not defile their garments--namely, the garments of their Christian profession, of which baptism is the initiatory seal, whence the candidates for baptism used in the ancient Church displayed in white. According to the Bible Eph 5:27, as to the spotlessness of the Church when she shall be presented to Christ; and Rev 19:8, as to the "fine linen, clean and white, the righteousness of the saints," in which it shall be granted to her to be dressed; and "the wedding garment."

Meanwhile, she is not to smear her Christian profession with any defilement of flesh or spirit but to "keep her garments." For no desecration shall enter the heavenly city. Not that any keep themselves here wholly free from defilement; but, as equated with worthless professors, the godly keep themselves unspotted from the world; and when they do contract it, they wash it away, to have their "robes white in the blood of the Lamb" (Rev 7:14). The Greek is not "to stain" but to "defile" or be smeared. **They shall walk with me in white**--The promised reward accords with the character of those to be rewarded: keeping their garments undefiled and white through the blood of the Lamb now, they shall walk with Him in while hereafter. On "with me," compare the exact words, Lu 23:43; Joh 17:24. "Walk" implies spiritual life, for only the living walk; also, emancipation, for it is only the free who walk at large. The grace and dignity of flowing long garments are seen to best advantage when the person "walks": so, the fineness of the saints reveals their character shall appear ultimately when they shall serve the Lord perfectly henceforth (Rev 22:3).

They are worthy with the worthiness (not their own, but that) which Christ has put on them (Rev 7:14). Eze 16:14, "perfect through MY charm which I had put upon thee." Grace is glory in the bud. "The worthiness here denotes a congruity between the saint's state of grace on earth, and that of glory, which the Lord has appointed for them, about to be projected by the law itself of grace" (Acts 13:46).

Therefore, white is not a dull white but a glittering, dazzling white. (Matt 13:43). The body transfigured into the likeness of Christ's body, and emanating beams of light displayed from Him, is probably the "white raiment" promised here.

The clothing is Greek, "garments." "He that overcomes" shall receive the same reward as they who "have not defiled their garments" (Rev 3:4). Therefore, the two are identical: "I will not by any means." blot out the name out of the book of life of the heavenly city. A register kept in ancient cities of their citizens: the names of the dead erased.

So those who have a name that they live and are dead (Rev 3:1) are blotted out of God's roll of the heavenly citizens and heirs of eternal life; not that in God's electing decree they ever were in His book of life.

But, according to human beliefs, those who had a high name for holiness would be supposed to be in it and were, concerning rights, actually among those in the way of salvation. Still, these privileges, and the fact that they once might have been saved, shall be of no avail to them. As to the book of life (Rev 13:8; 17:8; 20:12, 15; 21:27; Ex 32:32; Ps 69:28; Da 12:1). In the sense of the "called," many are enrolled among the called to salvation, who shall not be found among the chosen at last. The faint of salvation is more comprehensive than that of appointment. The appointment is fixed. Salvation is open to all and is pending humanity speaking in the case of those mentioned here. But (Rev 20:15; 21:27) exhibit the book of the elect alone in the narrower sense, after the erasure of the others.

In the presence of." the same promise of Christ's confessing before His Father those who confessed Him. (Matt 10:32, 33; Lu 12:8, 9). When you ignore "in heaven" after "My Father," because now that He is in heaven, there is no distinction between the Father in heaven and the Son on earth. He now sets His seal from heaven upon many of His words. An undersigned fluke, proving that these letters are, as they profess, in their words, as well as substance, Christ's addresses; not even tinged with the color of John's style, such as it appears in his Gospel and Epistles. The coincidence is mainly with the three other Gospels, not with John's, making the coincidence more markedly undersigned. So also, the clause, "He that hath an ear, let him hear," is not repeated in John's Gospel but from the Lord's own words in the three synoptic Gospels (Matt 11:15; 13:9; Mt 4:9, 23; 7:16; Lu 8:8; 14:35). Philadelphia in Lydia, twenty-eight miles southeast of Sardis, was built by Attalus, king of Pergamos, who died A.D. 138. It was destroyed by an earthquake in the reign of Tiberius.

The connection of this Church with Jews there causes the lecture to have an Old Testament coloring in the descriptions working. It and Smyrna alone of the seven receive authentic praise. As in the Old Testament, that is holy as in the Old Testament, "the Holy One of Israel." Jesus and the God of the Old Testament are one. None but God is holy and separate from evil and perfectly hating it.

In the synagogue of Satan" (Rev 3:9). Our God" distinguished from the false gods and from all those who say they are what they are not (Re 3:9): real, genuine. However, He perfectly realizes all that is involved in the names, GOD, Light (Joh 1:9; 1Jo 2:8), Bread (John 6:32), the Vine (Joh 15:1); as distinguished from all average, limited, and flawed insights of the idea. His nature answers to His name (John 17:3; 1Th 1:9). On the other hand, it is "truth-speaking" and "truth-loving" (Joh n3:33; Tit 1:2). The keys of David: Eliakim, the "keys," the symbol of authority "over the house of David," was transferred from Shebna, who was removed from the office of servant or treasurer, as unworthy of it.

Christ, the Heir of the throne of David, shall unseat all the less worthy guardians who have abused their trust in God's spiritual house, and "shall reign over the house of Jacob," literal and spiritual (Lu 1:32, 33)."Forever," "as a Son over His own house" (Heb 3:2-6). It rests with Christ to open or shut the heavenly palace, deciding who is and who is not, to be admitted: as He also opens, or shuts, the prison, having the keys of hell (the grave) and death (Re 1:18). The power of the keys was given to Peter and the other apostles only when, and in so far as, Christ made him and them trustworthy. Whatever degrees of this power may have been committed to ministers, the supreme power belongs to Christ alone. Thus, Peter rightly opened the Gospel door to the Gentiles (Acts 10:1-48; 11:17, 18; Acts 14:27). But he mistakenly tried to shut the door in part again (Ga 2:11-18). Eliakim had "the key of the house of David laid upon his shoulder": Christ, as the antitypical David, Himself has the key of the supreme "government upon His shoulder."

As in the former addresses, His attribute here accords with His promise. Though "the synagogue of Satan," false "Jews" (Re 3:9) try to "shut" the "door" which I "set open before thee"; "no man can shut it" (Rev 3). I have set "given": it is My gracious gift to the—open door for evangelization; a door of spiritual effectiveness. The opening of a door by Him to the Philadelphian Church accords with the previous assignation to Him of "the key of David. "Which no man can shut." However, "because in a little while this gives the idea that Christ says, He sets before Philadelphia an open door because she has some little strength; whereas the sense to some extent is he does so because he has "but little strength": being knowingly weak himself, he is the more substantial object for God's power to rest on that so the Lord Christ may have all the glory. He has kept the littleness of thy strength becoming the source of Almighty power to thee, as leading thee to rest entirely on our great power, thou hast kept My word. **"Little strength" means that she had a Church small in numbers and external resources: "a little flock poor in worldly goods, and of small account in the eyes of men."**

I prefer the view given above. "Thou did keep did not deny our name,":
alluding to some occasion when faithfulness was tested. I will make, **"I
make,"** accurately, "I give" (Rev 3:8). The promise to Philadelphia is
more significant than that to Smyrna. To Smyrna, the contract was that
"the synagogue of Satan" should not prevail against the faithful in her:
to Philadelphia, she should even win over some of "the synagogue of
Satan" to fall on their faces confess God is in his truth. Translate "some
of the synagogues." Christ shall come, and all Israel then be saved;
there is but "a remnant" gathered out of the Jews "according to the
election of grace." It is an instance of how Christ set before her an "open
door," some of her greatest adversaries, the Jews, being brought to the
obedience of the faith. Their worshipping before her feet expresses the
convert's willingness to take the very most minor place in the Church,
doing submissive honor to those whom once they persecuted, rather
than dwell with the ungodly. So, the Philippian jailer before Paul.

Patience"-endurance." "The word of our endurance" is our Gospel
word, which teaches patient endurance to expect my coming (Rev 1:9).
Our endurance is the endurance that we require and which we practice.

> Christ Himself now endures, patiently waiting until the
> usurper be cast out, and all "His enemies be made His footstool."
> So, too, His Church, for the joy before her of sharing His
> coming kingdom, endures patiently. Hence, (Rev 3:11) follows,
> **"Behold, I come quickly."** The reward is in kind: "because thou
> didst keep. "I also we will keep to that deliver thee out of," not to
> exempt from temptation. The hour of temptation--the appointed
> season of affliction and temptation the plagues were called "the
> temptations of Egypt"). The temptation": the sore temptation
> which is coming upon the time of great tribulation before Christ's
> second coming. (Det. 4:34). To try them that dwell upon the
> earth--those of land, earthy (Rev 8:13). "Dwell" implies that
> their home is earth, not heaven—all humanity, except the elect
> (Rev 13:8, 14).

The temptation brings out the faithfulness of those kept by Christ and toughens the doubting wrongdoers (Rev 9:20, 21; 16:11, 21). The persecutions which befell Philadelphia shortly after were sincere of the tremendous last tribulation before Christ's coming, to which the Church's awareness in all ages. Behold omitted by the three oldest manuscripts and most ancient versions. **I come quickly,** the great encouragement to enduring faithfulness and the reassurance under current trials. That which thou have **"The word of my patience," or "endurance"** (Rev 3:10), which He had just commended them for keeping, and which involved with it the reaching of the kingdom; this they would lose if they surrendered to the temptation of exchanging regularity and suffering for compromise and ease. That no man takes thy crown which then thou wouldst receive that no tempter cause thee to lose it: not that the tempter would thus secure it for himself (Col 2:18). In one sense, the pillar in the temple has "no temple" in the heavenly city because there shall be no difference between things sacred and secular, for all things and persons shall be holy to the Lord.

The city shall be all one great temple, in which the saints shall be not just stones, as the spiritual temple now on earth. Still, all distinguished as pillars: steadfastly firm unlike Philadelphia, the city which was so often surprised by earthquakes, like the massive pillars before Solomon's temple, Boaz that is, "In it is strength," and Jachin established": only that those pillars were outside, these shall be within the temple. Our God are stronger, never more at all. As the elect angels are beyond the possibility of falling, being now under "the blessed necessity of goodness," so shall the saints be. The door shall be shut and safely in forever the elect and shut out the lost (Matt 25:10; Joh 8:35 Isa 22:23, Rev 2:7). They shall be priests forever unto God (Rev 1:6). "Who would not yearn for that city out of which no friend departs and into which no enemy enters?

They were written upon him in the name of my God as belonging to God in a sense (Rev 7:3; 9:4; 14:1 Rev 22:4). Therefore, secure as the name of Jehovah ("Holiness to the Lord") was on the golden plate on the high priest's forehead (Ex 28:36-38); so the saints in their heavenly royal priesthood shall bear His name openly, as sacred to Him. The label is on the beast's followers (Rev 13:16, 17) and the harlot (Rev 17:5; Rev 20:4).

The name of the city of my God as one of its citizens (Re 21:2, 3, 10, Psalm 45). The full description of the town forms the correct close of the book. The saint's citizenship is now hidden, but it shall be manifested: he shall have the right to enter through the city's gates (Rev 22:14). It was the city of Abraham. It is not the old Jerusalem, once called "the holy city," but having forfeited the name. It would express that it had recently come into existence, but in Greek, "Kaine," which is new and different, displacing the worn-out old Jerusalem and its society. "John, in the Gospel, relates to the ancient city the Greek name Hierosolyma. But in Armageddon, always, the Hebrew name, Jerusalem, to the heavenly city. The Hebrew name is the original and holier one:

Our new name is beyond words and only known to God: to be in the future revealed and made the believer's own in union with God in Christ. Christ's name written on him indicates he shall ultimately be Christ's. New also relates to Christ, who shall accept a new character his "new name "entering with His saints on a kingdom, not that He had with the Father before the worlds, but that earned by his disgrace as Son of man.

His name gives an unwilling testimony to the fulfillment of the prophecy as to Philadelphia from a material point of view; among the Greek colonies and churches of Asia, Philadelphia is still erect --a column in a scene of ruins as an excellent example that the paths of honor and safety may sometimes be the same." Laodiceans, the city was in the southwest of Phrygia, on the river Lycus, not far from Colossi, and between it and Philadelphia. It was destroyed by an earthquake, A.D. 62 and rebuilt by its wealthy citizens without the help of the state. (Re 2:7). This wealth occurs from the quality of its wool. It led to a self-satisfied, lukewarm state in spiritual things, as Re 3:17, Col 4:16, on the Letter which is thought to have been written to the Laodicean Church by Paul.

The Church in latter times was prospering; one of the councils at which the principle of Scripture was determined was held in Laodicea in A.D. 361. Hardly a Christian is now to be found on or near its site. The Amen is (Isa 65:16, Hebrew, "Bless Himself in the God of Amen swear by Amen," 2Co 1:20). He who not only says but is the Truth. The saints used Amen at the end of the prayer or in assenting to the word of God, but none, save the Son of God, ever said, "Amen, I say unto you," for it is the foreign language unique to God, who declares by Himself. The New Testament formula, "Amen. I say unto you," parallels the Old Testament formula, "as I live, saith Jehovah." In John's Gospel alone, He uses in the Greek the double "Amen," John 1:51; 3:3, in Verily, indeed."

His unchanging faithfulness as **"the Amen"** separates with Laodicea's wavering of purpose, "neither hot nor cold" (Re 3:16). The angel of Laodicea has been assumed to be Archippus, to whom, thirty years earlier, Paul had already given a monition, as requiring to be stirred up to attentiveness in his ministry. So, they named him the first bishop of Laodicea: supposed to be the son of Philemon (Phil 2).

Faithful and true witness as **"the Amen"** expresses the unmovable truth of His promises; so "the faithful the true witness," the truth of His revelations as to the heavenly things He has seen and testifies. "Faithful," that is, trustworthy (2Ti 2:11, 13). "True" is here (not truth-speaking, but "perfectly realizing all that is understood in the name Witness" (1Ti 6:13). Three things are necessary for this:

- ❖ to have seen with His own eyes what He attests
- ❖ to be competent to relate it to others
- ❖ to be willing truthfully to do so.
- ❖ In Christ, all these conditions meet the beginning of God's creation--not he whom God created first, but as in Col 1:15-18, Col 1:15-18).

❖ The Beginner of all creation is creating technique. All designs would not be characterized as adoring him if he were but one of themselves. His being the Creator is a strong guarantee of His faithfulness as "the Witness and Amen."

We know neither cold nor "hot," plainly, "boiling," and "fervent" Ac 18:25; Ro 12:11; So, 8:6; Lu 24:32) requires that "cold" should here mean more than negatively cold; it is instead, positively icy cold: having never yet been warmed. The Laodiceans were in spiritual things cold comparatively but not as complex as the world outside and those who had never belonged to the Church.

The lukewarm state, if it is the transitional stage to a warmer, is a desirable state for a bit of religion, if accurate, is better than none; but most fatal when, as here, an abiding condition, for it is mistaken for a safe state (Re 3:17). It accounts for Christ's desire that they were cold rather than lukewarm. There would not be the same "danger of mixed cause and ignored the principle." Also, there is more hope for the "cold," those who are of the world and not yet warmed by the Gospel call; for, when called, they may become hot and fervent Christians: such did once-cold publicans, Zaccheus and Matthew, become. But the lukewarm has been brought within reach of the holy fire without being heated by it into fervor:

However, having a religion is enough to break the conscience in false security, but not belief enough to save the soul. (2Tim 4:10). Such were the nooses between two thoughts in Israel (1Ki 18:21; 2Ki 17:41; Mt 6:24). But **neither cold nor hot--So one oldest document read. But two oldest documents, "hot nor cold."** The adjectives are in the male, agreeing with the angel, not womanly, agreeing with the Church. The Lord directs the angel as the personification and representative of the Church. The chief minister is accountable for his flock if they have not faithfully warned its members.

We will 'say am about to," "I am ready to": I have it in my mind: graciously the possibility of the threat not being executed, if only they repent at once. His dealings with them will depend on theirs towards Him.

He will you spew thee out of my month reject-with righteous hostility, as Canaan spew out its inhabitants for their abominations. Physicians used lukewarm water to cause vomiting.

Cold and hot drinks were standard at feasts but never lukewarm. There were hot and cold springs near Laodicea. Self-sufficiency is the fatal danger of a lukewarm state (Rev. 3:15).

Thou say virtually and mentally, if not in so many words.

Increased with goods, "have become enriched," implying self-praise in self-acquired riches. The Lord alludes to Ho 12:8. The means on which they prided themselves were spiritual, though, doubtless, their spiritual self-sufficiency was much fostered by their worldly wealth. On the other hand, poverty of spirit is encouraged by poverty concerning earthly riches.

❖ Know not that thou above all others. The "thou "art the wretched one."

The word miserable is, So one of the oldest manuscripts reads. But two oldest manuscripts prefix "the." Translate "the wretched"; "the one especially to be pitied." From their assessment of themselves, how different from Christ's reckoning of men, **"I need nothing!"**

They began blindly, whereas Laodicea bragged of a deeper than common insight into heavenly things. They were not blind, else eye-salve would have been of no avail, but short-sighted—gentle and loving sarcasm. Take our advice, thou who fanciest thyself in need of nothing. Thou not in need of nothing, but art in lack of the most ordinary necessaries of existence. He graciously stoops to their modes of thought and speech:

Thou art a people ready to listen to any counsel as to how to buy to benefit; then, listen to My counsel "Counsellor," Isa 9:6, according to Paul's Epistle written to the neighboring Colosse and intended for the Laodicean Church also, Col 2:1, 3; 4:16, are hidden all the treasures of wisdom and knowledge. "Buy" does not imply that we can, by any work or merit of ours, purchase God's gift; nay, the very purchase of money consists of renouncing all self-righteousness, such as Laodicea had (Rev 3:17).

"Buy" at the cost of thine own self-sufficiency so Paul, Php 3:7, 8, and the giving up of all things, however dear to us, would prevent our receiving Christ's salvation as a gift, for example, self and worldly desires. We can buy without money and price. (Isa 55:1).

The source of "unsearchable riches" (Eph 3:8). Laodicea was a city of extensive money transactions

Some gold accurately, "fired and fresh from the fire," just fresh from the furnace, which has proved its purity and retains its bright gloss. Sterling's spiritual wealth, as contrasted with its counterfeit, in which Laodicea boasted itself. Having bought this gold, she will be no longer poor (Rev 3:17).

White raiment garments." Laodicea's wools were famous. Christ offers infinitely whiter raiment. As "gold tried in the fire" expresses faith tested by fiery trials: so "white raiment," Christ's righteousness assigned to the believer in justification and taught in consecration.

It is revealed," such as, at the last day, when everyone devoid of the wedding garment shall be discovered. In the East, to strip one, the notion of putting to open shame. So also, to clothe one with fine apparel is the image of doing him honor. Man can discover his guilt; God alone can cover it so that his nakedness shall not be manifested at last (Col 3:10-14). Blessed is he whose sin is so protected. **The hypocrite's shame may be manifested now; it must be so at last.**

Anoint with eye-salve--The oldest manuscripts read, eye-salve a roll of ointment to anoint thine eyes." Christ has for Laodicea an ointment far more precious than all the costly oils of the East. The look is here the conscience or inner light of the mind. According as it is sound and "single" or otherwise, the man sees aright spiritually or does not. The Holy Spirit's enthusiasm, like the ancient eye-salve's, first intellects with a guilty verdict of sin, then heals. He opens our eyes first to ourselves in our wretchedness, then to the Savior in His preciousness.

Warning: that the most sunken churches of the seven, namely, Sardis and Laodicea, are the ones in which alone are specified no opponents from without, nor heresies from within. The Church owes much to God's over-ruling Divine Intervention, which has made so often internal and external foes promote His cause by calling forth their powers in asserting the faith once delivered to the saints. Peace is dearly bought at the cost of spiritual sluggishness, where there is no importance enough felt in religion to argue about it at all. (Job 5:17; PR 3:11, 12; Heb 12:5, 6.). So, in the case of Manasseh (2Ch 33:11-13). As many all. "He scourged every son he received. And shalt thou be an exception? If excepted from suffering the scourge, thou art excepted from the number of the sons". It is an encouragement to Laodicea not to despair but to regard the rebuke as a token for good if they profit from it.

We love "Philo," the love of unwarranted affection, independent of any grounds for esteem in the object loved. But in the case of Philadelphia (Re 3:9), "I have loved thee with the love of admiration, founded on the judgment. (Joh 21:15-17).

He rebukes the stands first in the sentence strongly. In our dealings, so altogether unlike man's, in the case of all whom I love, rebuke. The verb as in Joh 16:8, "(the Holy Ghost) will convince rebuke unto conviction the world of sin. Chasten--"chastise." which means to instruct, **in the New Testament means to instruct by chastisement (Heb 12:5, 6).** *David s rebuked unto conviction when* *he cried, "I have sinned against the Lord"; the chastening followed when his child was taken from him (2Sa 12:13, 14). In the divine chastening, the sinner at the same time winces under the rod and learns righteousness.*

Be zealous habitually. Present tense in the Greek, of a lifelong course of zeal. The opposite of "lukewarm." The resonance marks this: Laodicea had not been "hot." Therefore, she is urged to "be zealous" both are obtained from the same verb, "to boil."

Repent: of an act to be once for all done and done at once. Stand waiting in wonderful condescension and long-suffering.

Knock-- (So 5:2). It further manifests His loving desire for the sinner's salvation. He who is Himself "the Door," and who bids us "knock" that it may be "opened unto" us, is first Himself to knock at the door of our hearts. If He did not strike first, we should never come to knock at His door. Compare So 5:4-6, which is alluded to here; the Spirit thus in Revelation sealing the canonicity of that mystical book.

The spiritual state of the bride there, between waking and sleeping, slow to open the door to her divine lover, answers to that of the lukewarm Laodicea here. "Love regarding men emptied humbled God; for He does not remain in His place and call to Himself the servant he loved. He comes down Himself to seek him, and He who is all-rich arrives at the lodging of the poor person, and with His voice intimates His yearning love, and seeks a similar return, and withdraws not when disowned, and is not impatient at the insult, and when persecuted still waits at the doors".

Our voice can appeal to the sinner not only with his hand providences knocking but with his voice; his word read or heard; or rather, His Spirit inwardly applying to man's spirit the lessons to be drawn from His providence and His word. If we refuse to answer His knocking at our door now, He will refuse to hear our knocking at His door hereafter. Concerning His second coming also, He is even now at the door, and we know not how soon He may strike: therefore, we should always be ready to open to Him immediately.

If any man hears--for man is not obliged by appealing force: Christ knocks, but does not break open the door, though the violent take heaven by the power of prayer (Mt 11:12): whosoever does hear, does so not of himself, but by the drawings of God's grace (Joh 6:44): repentance is Christ's gift (Ac 5:31). He draws, not drags. The Son of righteousness, like the natural sun, the moment that the door is opened, pours in His light, which could not previously find an entrance. (Psalm 118:19).

We will come into him--as I did to Zaccheus. Supper with him, and he with me wonderful exchange. "Dwelleth in me, and I in Him," Joh 6:56. Whereas ordinarily, the admitted guest tastes with the admitter, the divine guest becomes Himself the host, for He is the bread of life and the Giver of the marriage feast. Here again, He alludes to the imagery of So 4:16, where the Bride invites Him to eat pleasant fruits, even as He had first prepared a feast for her, "His fruit was sweet to my taste." Compare the same interchange, Joh 21:9-13, the dinner made up of the food that Jesus brought and those the disciples brought. The consummation of this blessed intercommunion shall be at the Marriage Supper of the Lamb, of which the Lord's Supper is the earnest and foretaste.

Sit with me in my throne (Re 2:26, 27; 20:6; Mt 19:28; 20:23; Joh 17:22, 24; 2Ti 2:12). The same whom Christ had just before threatened to spew out of His mouth is now offered a seat with Him on His throne! "The highest place is within reach of the lowest; the faintest spark of grace may be fanned into the mightiest flame of love."

His Father's, upon which He now sits, and has sat since His ascension, after His victory over death, sin, the world; upon this none can sit save God, and the God-man Christ Jesus, for it is the incommunicable prerogative of God alone. The throne which shall be peculiarly his as the once humbled and then glorified Son of man, to be set up over the whole earth here to fore commandeered by Satan at his coming again; in this, the victorious saints shall share (1Co 6:2). The transfigured elect Church shall with Christ judge and reign over the nations in the flesh, and Israel the foremost of them; ministering blessings to them as angels were the Lord's mediators of benefit and administrators of His government in setting up His throne in Israel at Sinai. This privilege of our high calling belongs solely to the present time, while Satan reigns when there is scope for conflict and victory (2Ti 2:11, 12). When Satan shall be bound (Re 20:4), there shall be no more extended scope for it, for all on earth shall know the Lord from the least to the greatest. The grandest and crowning agreement was placed at the end of all the seven addresses to gather.

It also forms the link to the next part of the book, where the Lamb is introduced, seated on the right side of his father's throne (Rev 4:2, 3; 5:5, 6). The Eastern throne is broad, admitting others besides him who, as chief, occupy the center.

Warning: The order of the promises in the seven epistles corresponds to that of the unfolding of the kingdom of God from its first beginnings on earth to its consummation in heaven. To the faithful at Ephesus: The tree of life in the Paradise of God is promised (Rev 2:7), Ge 2:9). Sin entered the world and death by evil, but to the faithful, at Smyrna, it is promised that they shall not be hurt by the second death (Rev 2:11). The promise of the hidden manna (Rev 2:17) to Pergamos brings us to the Mosaic period, the Church in the wilderness. That to Thyatira, namely, triumph over the nations (Rev 2:26, 27), forms the kingdom's consummation in prophetic type, the period of David and Solomon characterized by this power of the countries.

Here there is a division, the seven falling into two groups, four and three, as often, for example, the Lord's Prayer, three and four. The scenery of the last three passes from earth to heaven, the Church contemplated as triumphant, with its steps from glory to glory. Christ promises to the believer of Sardis not to blot his name out of the book of life but to confess him before His Father and the angels on the judgment day and clothe him with a glorified body of dazzling whiteness (Rev 3:4, 5). To the faithful at Philadelphia, Christ promises they shall be citizens of the new Jerusalem, fixed as immovable pillars there, where city and temple are one (Rev 3:12).

Here, individual salvation is agreed to the believer, as in the case of Sardis, and privileges in the blessed communion of the Church are triumphant. Lastly, the faithful of Laodicea was given the crowning promise, not only the two former blessings but a seat with Christ on His throne, even as He has sat with His Father on His Father's throne (Rev 3:21).

CHAPTER 8

God's Righteous Judgment

Having exhibited the sinfulness of the immoral pagan in the chapter (1:18-32), Paul presents his case against the religious moralist, Jew or Gentile, by cataloging six principles that govern God's judgment.

❖ Knowledge (verse 1)
❖ Truth (verses 2-3)
❖ Guilt (verses 4-5)
❖ Deeds (verses 6-10)
❖ Impartiality (verses 11-15)
❖ Motive (verse 16).

*Romans 2:1 **"Therefore thou art inexcusable,** O man, whosoever thou art that judges: wherein thou judge another, thou condemn thyself; for thou that judges do the same things."*

It is straightforward for us to see sin in others' lives when we are often unable to see the same sin in our own lives.

Many ministers have the attitude that they are exempt because they preach. The same law applies to us all.

There are not two sets of rules:

❖ one for the congregation and one for the preacher. **"All have sinned and come short of the glory of God."**
❖ Everyone needs Jesus as Savior and Lord.

Both Jews who were Paul's primary audience here and moral Gentiles who think they are exempt from God's judgment because they have not indulged in the immoral overindulgences in chapter 1 are tragically mistaken. They have more knowledge than the immoral pagan and thus greater accountability.

"Condemn thyself:" If someone has enough knowledge to judge others, he condemns himself because he shows he knows to evaluate his condition. "Does the same things:" In their condemnation of others, they have excused and overlooked their sins.

Self-righteousness: exists because of two deadly errors. *Minimizing God's moral standard :*

❖ usually by emphasizing externals; and
❖ You are underestimating the depth of one's sinfulness.

Romans 2:2 "But we are sure that the judgment of God is according to truth against them which commit such things."

God will not punish anyone on hearsay evidence. God judges in Truth. He knows what the Truth is even before we begin.

"According to the truth": The meaning is 'right." Whatever God does, is by nature right.

Romans 2:3 "And thinks thou this, O man, that judges' them which do such things, and does the same, that thou shalt escape the judgment of God?"

"Condemn thyself:" If someone has enough knowledge to judge others, he condemns himself because he shows he knows to evaluate his condition.

Romans 2:4 "Or despises thou the riches of his goodness and forbearance and longsuffering; not knowing that the goodness of God leadeth thee to repentance?"

"*Despises*": Meaning to despise or think down on, thus underestimating someone's or something's value and even treating with contempt. "*Goodness*" refers to "common grace," the benefits God bestows on all men. "*Forbearance*": "to hold back" was sometimes used as a truce between warring parties. God graciously holds back His judgment rather than destroying every person when they sin. He saves sinners physically and temporally from what they deserve to show them. The saving character that they might come to Him and receive spiritual and eternal salvation.

"Longsuffering:" This word indicates the duration for which God demonstrates His goodness and forbearance for long periods.

Together these three words speak of God's common grace and how He demonstrates His grace to all humanity.

"Repentance": Turning from sin to Christ for forgiveness and salvation.

Romans 2:5 "But after thy hardness and impenitent heart treasures up unto thyself wrath against the day of wrath and revelation of the righteous judgment of God.

The English word **"sclerosis," as in arteriosclerosis, a hardening of the arteries,** comes from the Greek word. But here, the danger is not physical, **but spiritual hardness.** "*Impenitent heart*": A refusal to repent and accept God's pardon of sin through Jesus and cling to one's wrong is to accumulate more of God's wrath and earn a severer judgment. **"Day of wrath ... judgment":** Refers to the final judgment of wicked men that comes at the Great White Throne at the end of the Millennium.

Warning: Although Scripture everywhere teaches that salvation is not based on works, it constantly teaches that God's judgment is always based on a man's deeds.

Paul describes the deeds of two distinct groups: the redeemed in verses 7 and 10 and the unredeemed as shown in 8-9. The acts of the redeemed are not the basis of their salvation but their evidence. **They are not perfect and are prone to sin, but there is undeniable evidence of righteousness in their lives.**

Romans 2:6 "Who will render to every man according to his deeds:"

We are all storing up things in heaven now. Some who walk in the Light of Jesus store up good treasures in heaven.

Matthew 6:19-21 "Lay not up for yourselves treasures upon earth, where moth and rust doth corrupt, and where thieves break through and steal:" "But lay up for yourselves treasures in heaven, where neither moth nor rust doth corrupt, and where thieves do not break through nor steal:" "For where your treasure is, there will your heart be also."

If our deeds are evil, the wrath of God will be our just payment. If we are working for God, only a warm welcome awaits us, and the statement, well done thy good and faithful servant. In (verse 7), we see the rewards awaiting the believer.

Romans 2:7 "To them who by patient continuance in well-doing seek for glory and honor and immortality, eternal life:"

Notice that even though eternal life is a gift, we must continue walking in the salvation Jesus has provided for us. We must continue walking in the Light. We must be doing the Word and not just hearing the Word. Verse seven is not simply speaking in duration because even unbelievers will live forever, but also in quality. Eternal life is a kind of life, the holy life that the everlasting God has given to believers. We see (verse 8) what awaits those who are not walking with Jesus in His Light.

Romans 2:8 "But unto them that are contentious, and do not obey the truth, but obey unrighteousness, anger, and wrath, "God is not unaware. He will punish those who do not follow. From Genesis to Revelation, we see blessings for those who live for God and curses for those who are the children of disobedience. Romans 2:9-10 "Tribulation and anguish, upon every soul of man that doeth evil, of the Jew first, and of the Gentile;" "But glory, honor, and peace, to every man that worketh good, to the Jew first, and the Gentile." Just as the Jews were given the first opportunity to hear and respond to the gospel, they will be the first to receive God's judgment if they refuse. Israel will receive sterner punishment because she was given more excellent light and blessing.

Romans 2:11 "For there is no respect of persons with God."

God is not impressed with our worldly wealth, importance, position in the church, Title in the church, influence, popularity, or appearance. We are what we are because God chose it to be that way. If you are jealous of someone's wealth or place in society, blame God.

The real reason might be that God could not trust you with the wealth or importance. It might even be for your good. We do not even choose our nationality; God does. We were born and raised in a particular family because God arranged it. Why should anyone be so proud of themselves, this being the case? The only wealth that amounts to anything is what we have stored in heaven.

Romans 2:12 "For as many as have sinned without law shall also perish without law: and as many as have sinned in the law shall be judged by the law."

"Sinned without law": The Gentiles who never had the opportunity to know God's moral law will be judged on their disobedience to their limited knowledge as we studied (Romans 1:19-20). "Sinned in the law": The Jews and many Gentiles who had access to God's moral law will be accountable for their more excellent knowledge.

To those to whom much is given, much is required.

Luke 12:48: "But he that knew not, and did commit things worthy of stripes, shall be beaten with few stripes. For unto whom much is given, of him shall be much required: and to whom men have committed much, they will ask the more."The Lord is a just God. He judges each according to their knowledge. If we know to do good and do it not, it is counted as sin.

3 John 1:11 "Beloved, follow not that which is evil, but that which is good. He that doeth good is of God: but he that doeth evil hath not seen, God."

We mentioned before that even nature tells you of God. Our conscience tells us when we are sinning. We all know right from wrong. The Jew had the law, so they would be judged by their law if they did not receive Jesus. All will be deemed guilty of sin who have not accepted complete pardon through Jesus Christ our Lord. All deserve death. We receive our life in Jesus Christ, who is Life.

Romans 2:13 "For not the hearers of the law are just before God, but the doers of the law shall be justified."

Just hearing the law and doing nothing about it would not help at all, or just hearing about Jesus will not save you either. We must act upon what we hear. The burden is on the person receiving salvation to accept it. We have free will, which God will not violate.

Romans 10:9-10 "That if thou shalt confess with thy mouth the Lord Jesus and believe in your heart that God hath raised him from the dead, thou shalt be saved." "For with the heart man believeth unto righteousness, and with the mouth, the confession made unto salvation."

Romans 2:14 "For when the Gentiles, which have not the law, do by nature the things contained in the law, these, having not the law, are a law unto themselves:"

Without knowing the written law of God, people in pagan society generally value and attempt to practice its most basic doctrines. It is usual for cultures automatically value justice, honesty, compassion, and goodness toward others, reflecting the divine law written in the heart. "Law unto themselves": Their practice of some good deeds and their distaste for some evil one's validation of a natural knowledge of God's law, an understanding that will witness against them on the day of judgment.

Romans 2:15 "Which shows the law's work written in their hearts, their conscience also bearing witness, and their thoughts mean while accusing or else excusing one another.

"*Work of the law*": Probably best understood as "the same works the Mosaic law prescribes. "*Conscience*": Literal meaning "with knowledge." That natural sense of right and wrong produces guilt when violated. In addition to an essential awareness of God's law, men have a warning system that activates when they choose to ignore or disobey that law.

Paul urges believers not to violate their consciences or cause others to because repeatedly ignoring the conscience's warnings dull them and eventually silences them.

CHAPTER 9

Irresponsible Shepherds

Ezekiel Chapter 34

Ezekiel 34:1 "And the word of the LORD came unto me, saying, "This again is a brand-new prophecy. Ezekiel turns from the people to their leaders, who have the most significant guilt.

From this chapter on, Ezekiel's messages are primarily comforting, telling of God's grace and faithfulness to His covenant promises.

Ezekiel 34:2 "Son of man, prophesy against the shepherds of Israel, prophesy, and say unto them, thus saith the Lord GOD unto the shepherds; Woe be to the shepherds of Israel that do feed themselves! should not the shepherds feed the flocks?" Prophesy against the shepherds of Israel":

The reference was to pre-exilic leaders such as kings, priests, prophets, civil leaders, and their spiritual leaders, which means those false ones who swindled the flock for personal gain (verses 3-4) rather than fed or led righteously. It stands in conflict with the Lord as Shepherd. These Scriptures have a meaning for the Jews and the Christians. We will look at both. The very beginning of these verses is a reprimand for not caring for the sheep. The kings then and the preachers must be careful to feed the sheep. That is the primary job of a shepherd.

Ezekiel 34:3 "Ye eat the fat, and ye clothe you with the wool, ye kill them that are fed: but ye feed not the flock."

The scripture speaks of those who take from the sheep and give nothing. In some churches today, we see that ministers are living far above the conditions of their people and are not teaching them true doctrine or the dangers of not living according to God's holy word.

Ezekiel 34:4 "The diseased have ye not strengthened, neither have ye healed that which was sick, neither have ye bound up that which was broken, neither have ye brought again that which was driven away, neither have ye sought that which was lost; but with force and with cruelty have ye ruled them."

Some treat the church as a hotel for saints and not a hospital for sinners.

Mark 2:17 "When Jesus heard this, he saith unto them, they that are whole have no need of the physician, but they that are sick: I came not to call the righteous, but sinners to repentance."

Those whose spirits are sick need us. The weak sheep need more care than the healthy ones. A good shepherd keeps his sheep together with love, patience, and kindness, not by driving them. Jesus told the parable about the shepherd that left the ninety-nine and went to find that one that was lost. The 23rd Psalm describes the good Shepherd.

Ezekiel 34:5 "And they were scattered because there is no shepherd: and they became meat to all the beasts of the field when they were scattered."

When the flock is divided, it is easy prey for the wolves. They get one sheep off from the others and kill him. It is true of the church. Together we stand, divided we fall. The wolf is not afraid of the sheep, but he is scared of the shepherd. The shepherd drives the wolf away and saves the sheep.

In verse above, there is no shepherd. The sheep are easy prey. Therefore, a Christian needs fellowship in a church with other Christians and under the care of a pastor. There is safety in the numbers, and the pastor protects the single-member. The pastor is a protector and teacher. The beasts of the field pictured here picture the nations that prey on Israel (Dan. 7:3-7), though it could include actual wild beasts (14:21, 34:25, and 28).

Ezekiel 34:6 "My sheep wandered through all the mountains, and upon every high hill: yea, my flock was scattered upon all the face of the earth, and none did search or seek after them."

To hold a civil office or an office in a church carries a severe responsibility. We should not take office if we have not weighed the cost and are willing to sacrifice to do a good job. The loss of the world today is like those sheep on the mountains. We must go and get them.

Being saved is terrific, but God called His workers to seek out the lost. How can they be saved without hearing the word? They must listen to the Word of God to be saved.

Ezekiel 34:7 "Therefore, ye shepherds, hear the word of the LORD."

This is not just an idle statement but **a warning** to today's ministers and the leaders of the churches.

Ezekiel 34:8 "As I live, saith the Lord GOD, surely because my flock became a prey, and my flock became meat to every beast of the field because there was no shepherd, neither did my shepherds search for my flock, but the shepherds fed themselves, and fed not my flock."

All who work in the ministry should be ministering because God called them to that task, not as a way of making a living. Of course, you must have a living, but it should not be your reason for accepting a specific job. The food that the minister of God must bring the flock is the pure Word of God. The Word cannot be watered down, or it will not nourish the sheep. The sheep will not be in much danger of straying away when they are well fed. When they know the Word of God, they are not as quickly drawn away to false prophets.

Ezekiel 34:9 "Therefore, O ye shepherds, hear the word of the LORD;" This is no idle threat, as proven by the case of King Zedekiah (Jer. 52:10-11).

Ezekiel 34:10 "Thus saith the Lord GOD; Behold, I am against the shepherds; and I will require my flock at their hand and cause them to cease from feeding the flock; neither shall the shepherds feed themselves anymore; for I will deliver my flock from their mouth, that they may not be meat for them."

God will not allow a leader to go on who does not care for the people. Those shepherds, who do not care for the sheep, will be replaced by some who care for the sheep. The owner, God, does not want to lose his sheep. The keyword in the verse above is mouth. He will deliver them from his mouth. These are words he is providing them. The false prophet will say anything to enrich his pocket. He is not interested in the sheep. They have not brought God's message to these people so that God will require them at the false prophet's hand.

CHAPTER 10

God's, The True Shepherd

Ezekiel 34:11 "For thus saith, the Lord GOD; Behold, I, even I, will search my sheep, and seek them out."

God will search for Israel out and restore her to her homeland. God, the true Shepherd, would search out and find His sheep to restore Israel to their land for the kingdom which the Messiah leads.

Ezekiel 34:12 "As a shepherd seek out his flock in the day that he is among his sheep that are scattered; so, will I seek out my sheep and deliver them out of all places where they have been scattered in the cloudy and dark day."

It is specifically speaking of the house of Israel, which is scattered as captives in foreign lands. It is also speaking of the Lord bringing His sheep into the church.

Acts 2:17 "And it shall come to pass in the last days, saith God, I will pour out of my Spirit upon all flesh: and your sons and your daughters shall prophesy, and your young men shall see visions, and your old men shall dream dreams:"

"A cloudy and dark day" refers to the "day of the Lord" judgment on Israel.

Ezekiel 34:13 "And I will bring them out from the people, gather them from the countries, bring them to their own land, feed them upon the mountains of Israel by the rivers, and in all the inhabited places of the country."

Babylon will be destroyed, and God's people will come home to their Promised Land. It is God who frees them. The land of Israel will again be a land of milk and honey. With God's blessings upon it, it will flourish.

Verses 12-14: Here is the promise of a precise regathering and restoration of the people of Israel to their land from their worldwide spreading.

Since the scattering was precise, the regathering must also be distinct. Once they are regathered in Messiah's kingdom, they will no longer want (verses 15-16).

Ezekiel 34:14 "I will feed them in a good pasture, and upon the high mountains of Israel shall their fold be: there shall they lie in a good fold, and in a fat pasture shall they feed upon the mountains of Israel."

It is speaking of the beautiful pastureland where the shepherds tended their sheep. The 23rd Psalm gives an excellent example of what this Scripture says. Israel will be restored to their God and His protection and be restored to their land. The land would be no good without the blessings of God upon it.

Ezekiel 34:15 "I will feed my flock, cause them to lie down, saith the Lord GOD."

The "lying down" speaks of peace. God brings them peace, as well as supplying their needs. He feeds their bodies and spirits. It will happen because God promised it.

It is like the grace that He gives the Christian. **"Grace" means unmerited favor**. It is what they received, and the Christian receives as well.

Ezekiel 34:16 "I will seek that which was lost, and bring again that which was driven away, and bind up that which was broken, and strengthen that which was sick: but I will destroy the fat and the strong; **I will feed them with judgment."**

The **"fat"** in the Scripture speaks of the shepherd who took everything for himself: the fat and the strong speak of those who have abused others to get what they wanted. The sick and broken are speaking of those who needed a Savior. It is that judgment day when God separates the sheep which belong to Him from the goats.

In contrast to self-indulgent leaders who took advantage of the sheep, God will meet the needs of His people sheep. It is reminiscent of the 23rd Psalm.

Verses 17-22: Once He has judged the leaders, God will also judge **the abusive members of the flock** as to their actual spiritual state. This passage anticipates the judgment of the people given by Jesus Christ in **Matthew 25:31-46,** where Christ separates the sheep from the goats.

Ezekiel 34:17 "And as for you, O my flock, thus saith the Lord GOD; Behold, I judge between cattle and cattle, between the rams and he-goats."

- ❖ **"Behold, I judge between**
- ❖ **Cattle and cattle- older saints & younger saints. (Righteous saints).**
- ❖ **Female and male goats are between the sheep and he-goats"- female & male's goats (rebellious saints).**
- ❖ **Between the smaller and weaker cattle- newborn sheep & sick sheep.**
- ❖ **The sheep and the lambs- older saints and newborn -saints.**
- ❖ **And the more prominent and more vital cattle, "the rams and he-goats"- the righteous and unrighteous.**

By which the latter may be meant persons of superior power and authority. At least in their vanities, they are of more incredible wealth and riches and more wisdom and knowledge.

And who were oppressive and harmful to the poor and ordinary people, and less knowing, at least as they thought. Now, as he observed a difference between them, the Lord would make this known and take the part of the one against the other. Even the part of the weaker against, the more potent.

Ezekiel 34:18 "Seem it a small thing unto you to have eaten up the good pasture, but ye must stomp down with your feet the scum of your pastures? and have drunk of the deep waters, but ye must dirty the scum with your feet?"

Shepherds had taken big salaries, lived in huge homes, and driven expensive cars when their people were barely scraping a living. They had taken the best for themselves and let some of their people go hungry.

Ezekiel 34:19 "And as for my flock, they eat that which ye have trodden with your feet; and they drink that which ye have contaminated with your feet."

They have fed the flock with messages they had spoiled. They had changed the food God provided. They have trampled on the Word of God. Then, they fed it to the sheep.

Ezekiel 34:20 "Therefore thus saith the Lord God, unto them; Behold, I, even I, will judge between the fat cattle and the lean cattle."

On judgment day, the judgment is just because Jesus is the Righteous Judge.

Ezekiel 34:21 "Because ye have pushed with side and with shoulder, and pushed all the diseased with your horns, till ye have scattered them abroad;."

It is pure and straightforward oppression of the rich over the poor. It could be those in high authority taking advantage of those of low estate.

It would be those who are poor being removed from migrant churches. **"Horns" symbolize power.**

Ezekiel 34:22 "Therefore will I save my flock, and they shall no more be a prey, and I will judge between cattle and cattle."

It says the cattle and cattle, which means they are supposed to be Israelites all. Some will be saved, and some will not. It also is speaking of those who call themselves Christians. Not all who call themselves Christians will be saved.

Matthew 7:21 "Not everyone that saith unto me, Lord, Lord, shall enter into the kingdom of heaven; but he that doeth the will of my Father which is in heaven."

Ezekiel 34:23 "And I will set up one shepherd over them, and he shall feed them, even my servant David; he shall feed them, and he shall be their shepherd."

It is speaking of that great Shepherd, the Lord Jesus Christ.

John 10 1:18, we see who the servant David mentioned here is. I will give just one verse. Jesus calls Himself the Good Shepherd in the next verse.

John 10:11 "I am the good shepherd: the good shepherd giveth his life for the sheep."

Read all of it to get a fuller idea. Jesus is that One Shepherd. His genuine concern was for His sheep.

Ezekiel 34:24 "And I the Lord will be their God, and my servant David a prince among them; I the Lord have spoken it."

It is speaking of God the Father. Jesus opened the way to the Father for each of us when He gave His body on the cross. The veil in the temple in Jerusalem rent from the top to the bottom, giving all believers in Christ access to the Father.

Christ took on Himself the form of a servant on the earth. He is that promised King that will reign forever. Jesus Christ purchased us with His precious blood, and we are now sons of God if we believe.

Romans 8:14-15 "For as many as are led by the Spirit of God; they are the sons of God." "For ye have not received the spirit of bondage again to fear, but ye have received the Spirit of adoption, whereby we cry, Abba, Father."

Ezekiel 34:25 "And I will make with them a covenant of peace and will cause the evil beasts to cease out of the land: and they shall dwell safely in the wilderness, and sleep in the woods."

The covenant of peace is a gift offered to man. The old covenant collapsed because humanity did not obey God. The new covenant is the covenant of grace. We remember how Israel had trouble during the siege with the wild animals. There will now be peace. God provides their safety. It is speaking of actual animals that will be tamed in the kingdom (Isaiah 11:6-9; 35:9 and Hosea 2:18).

Ezekiel 34:26 "And I will make them and the places around my hill a blessing, and I will cause the shower to come down in his season; there shall be showers of blessing."

It is a character reference to Jerusalem and Zion, where the Jews will come to worship the Lord. **"Showers of blessing":** The "times of refreshing" (in Acts 3:19-20), when the curses of (Deut. 28:15-68).

God controls the elements. It rains when He tells it to. The blessings of God are now upon them, so the rain and the sunshine will come just at the right time for the crops to flourish. All good gifts come from God.

Ezekiel 34:27 "And the tree of the field shall yield her fruit, and the earth shall yield her increase, and they shall be safe in their land, and shall know that I am the Lord when I have broken the bands of their yoke and delivered them out of the hand of those that served themselves of them."

God's blessings are back upon them. God will again be their protection. They are His people, and He will pour blessing on them as He has done in the past. His anger is gone. He loves them as a Father loves a son. The faithfulness of the land is also indicated (in Amos 9:13).

Ezekiel 34:28 "And they shall no more be a prey to the heathen, neither shall the beast of the land devour them; but they shall dwell safely, and none shall make them afraid."

The enemy will not come against them now because the enemy is afraid of Israel's God. The only time the beasts, or the heathen, could attack them before was when God took His protection away. His safety is back now. They are His people, and He is their God. God will stop other nations from defeating the people of Israel.

Ezekiel 34:29 "And I will raise a plant of renown for them, and they shall be no more consumed with hunger in the land, neither bear the shame of the heathen anymore."

The "plant of renown" could have spoken of Jesus as the Branch. It could also be speaking of the abundant food supply they would have now that they are back in good graces with God. Many had starved during the famine when Babylon attacked them. There will be plenty to eat now.

Ezekiel 34:30 "Thus shall they know that I the LORD their God am with them and that they, even the house of Israel, are my people, saith the Lord GOD."

They were His people, even when they were in captivity in Babylon. He was chastising them as a Father does a misbehaving child. They had been unfaithful. Now, all is forgotten. God has forgiven them and taken them back. The Lord their God": An oft-repeated Old Testament theme. It speaks of the ultimate salvation of Israel (Romans 11:25-27).

Ezekiel 34:31 "And ye my flock, the flock of my pasture, are men, and I am your God, saith the Lord GOD. "This leaves no doubt that the sheep were speaking of God's people. They must choose to be His people, and He will be their God.

CHAPTERS 11

Abomination in the Temple

Ezekiel Chapter 8

Ezekiel 8:1 "And it came to pass in the sixth year, in the sixth month, in the fifth day of the month, as I sat in mine house, and the elders of Judah sat before me, that the hand of the Lord GOD fell there upon me."

The sixth month is about the same time as September. It begins a new vision. Notice that the hand of God touches Ezekiel. It is a year and one month after Ezekiel's first vision at Chebar.

Ezekiel is in his home when this latest vision comes. The elders of Judah, possibly, were some of the few who still believed in Ezekiel. The war had worsened, and so had the idolatry. The false prophets were promising the fall of Babylon soon. The people would rather hear their news than listen to Ezekiel and realize this cause them to repent.

Chapters 8-11 though the subject matter may be divided. These chapters represent a vision that the prophet had while transported by the Spirit of God from Babylon to Jerusalem (verse 3).

Ezekiel witnessed the presence of disgusting, idolatrous figures and cruel pagan practices within the temple, restricting itself **to "the wicked abominations"** (verse 9).

Ezekiel 8:2 "Then I beheld, and lo a likeness as the appearance of fire: from the appearance of his loins even downward, fire; and from his loins even upward, as the appearance of brightness, as the color of amber."

The color "amber" is the color of bronze and symbolizes judgment. The fire indicates the presence of God.

Thus, Daniel saw the Glory of God (Chapter 1: 26-28).

Ezekiel 8:3 "And he put forth the form of a hand and took me by a lock of mine head; and the spirit lifted me between the earth and the heaven and brought me in the visions of God to Jerusalem, to the door of the inner gate that looks toward the north; **where the seat of the image of jealousy, which provokes to jealousy."**

This mighty hand of God has reached down and miraculously snatched Ezekiel in the spirit, into the heavens, directly above the earth. This vision causes Ezekiel to see inside the inner gate that looks to the north. The word that **"seat" was translated from indicates the number of people.** God's presence was in the temple in the smoke and fire. **"Image," here, is speaking of likeness.** God is looking at this false god sitting on His throne. **It stirred up the jealousy of Almighty God. God's name is Jealous.**

Exodus 34:14 "For thou shalt worship no other god: for **the Lord, whose name is Jealous, He is a jealous God:"**

The north often speaks of power, majesty, judgment, direction, gloom, and God 's throne. Ezekiel is the reason for God bringing judgment against the people and on the temple. These visions are not a description of deeds done in the past in Israel, but a review of Israel's present condition, as they occurred at that time.

Ezekiel 8:4 "And behold, the glory of the God of Israel was there, according to the vision that I saw in the plain."

"The Glory of the God": Presence of God; God was also there in glory but was ignored while the people worshipped the idols (verse 6).

This vision is of the presence of God in the temple before its destruction. God is showing Ezekiel the reason for His departure from the temple and the temple's destruction. He had every reason to destroy these people. They were His wives, and they had played the harlot by worshipping false gods.

Ezekiel 8:5 "Then said he unto me, Son of man, lift your eyes toward the north. So, I lifted my eyes the way toward the north and beheld northward at the altar gate this image of jealousy in the entry."

God had not abandoned the people. His presence had been in the temple. They had forsaken God.

Ezekiel 8:6 "he said furthermore unto me, Son of man, see thou what they do? Even the great abominations that the house of Israel committed here, I should go far off from my temple? but turn you yet again, and thou shalt see greater abominations."

"That I should go far off from my temple": Sin would expel the people from their land and God from His temple.

They had made idols of silver, gold, and wood. Some of them had been in the temple itself, in the very presence of God. They were a constant reminder to God of their unfaithfulness. Their lack of faith in God has driven God away from His temple, where He met with His people. **His anger has risen in His face.**

Ezekiel 8:7 "And he brought me to the court door; and when I looked, behold a hole in the wall."

A gate that led to the outer court and the priests' rooms and their families. The seventy members of the Sanhedrin lived.

Ezekiel 8:8 "Then said he unto me, Son of man, dig now in the wall: and behold a door when I dig in the wall."

It appears that this was a hidden area in the wall of the rooms. There seemed to be a secret door show the clandestine secrecy of these idolaters, practicing their cult in hiding.

Ezekiel 8:9 "And he said unto me, go in, and behold the wicked abominations that they do here."

It was not in the central part of the temple but in the places, they stayed near the temple. It warns all who minister the Word of God to make sure their private lives are holy and their public lives.

In the private lives of the priests and the high priest, they were worshipping false gods. **"Abominations" are revolting sins in the sight of God.**

Ezekiel 8:10 "So I went in and saw, and behold every form of creeping thing, and abominable beasts, and all the idols of the house of Israel, described upon the wall round about."

The temple's walls are ugly, with drawings showing animals linked with Egyptian animal cults and other idols. Leaders of Israel, who should be worshipping the temple's God, are offering incense to them.

The people of God have undoubtedly picked up the culture of the heathen nations around them.

Ezekiel 8:11 "And there stood before them seventy men of the ancients of the house of Israel, and in the midst of them stood Jaazaniah the son of Shaphan, with every man his censer in his hand; and a thick cloud of incense went up."

The ancient men, who had been so dedicated to God in the past, are now seen burning incense to these false gods. These elders are not the Sanhedrin since it was not formed until after the restoration from Babylon, though the pattern had been much earlier. These men were appointed to guard against idolatry! Jaazaniah was the leader of the seventy. If he was the son of the Shaphan who read God's Word to Josiah (2 kings 22:8-11), we have some idea of the depth of sin to which the leaders had fallen.

Ezekiel 8:12 "Then said he unto me, Son of man, have thou seen what the ancients of the house of Israel do in the dark, every man in the chambers of his imagery? for they say, The Lord sees us not; the Lord has not forsaken the earth."

These seventy men thought because they were doing this in the privacy of their quarters, that God would not know what they were doing. They are blaming God for forsaking the earth when they have forsaken God. They have been unfaithful to God.

Ezekiel 8:13 "He also said unto me, turn thee yet again, and thou shalt see greater abominations that they do."

It is bad enough to cause the wrath of God to descend upon them; now, God says there are even worse things going on.

Ezekiel 8:14 "Then he brought me to the door of the gate of the Lord's house which is toward the north; and behold, there sat women weeping for Tammuz."

Yet a more incredible abomination than the secret cult was Israel's engaging in the Babylonian worship of Tammuz or Dumuzi, beloved of Ishtar, the god of spring vegetation. Vegetation burned in the summer, died in the winter, and came to life in the spring.

In July, the women mourned over the god's death and longed for his revival. The fourth month of the Hebrew calendar still bears the name Tammuz. With the worship of this idol were the vilest immoralities.

Weeping for Tammuz was an act of worship expected to bring him back from the netherworld. Thus, these women were worshipping this Assyrian deity.

Ezekiel 8:15 "Then said he unto me, has thou seen this, O son of man? turn thee yet again, and thou shalt see greater abominations than these."

It is almost impossible to believe there could be anything worse than this, but there is. God is bringing Ezekiel's attention to all the sins to show why He destroyed them. God was justified in His judgment; He wants Ezekiel to understand that justification.

Ezekiel 8:16 "And he brought me into the inner court of the Lord's house, and behold, at the door of the temple of the Lord, between the porch and the altar, about five and twenty men, with their backs toward the temple of the Lord, and their faces toward the east; and they worshipped the sun toward the east."

The twenty-five worshipped the false sun god, which is as old as history. The Son of God, Jesus, is the Light of the world. The worship of the sun is counterfeit of prayer to the true God. The sun is nothing. It is just a container for the light. Jesus Christ is the Light of the world. These twenty-five men were representative of the twenty-four priests and the High Priest, which make up the twenty-five. This is convincing because they were in the most sacred inner court where only priests could go. It was an insult to God.

Ezekiel 8:17 "Then he said unto me, has thou seen this, O son of man? Is it a light thing to the house of Judah that they commit the abominations which they commit here? for they have filled the land with violence and have returned to provoke me to anger: and, lo, they put the branch to their nose."

The "putting off the branch to their nose" was part of the sacred worship of the false sun god. It seems to have been some act of contempt toward God.

The worst part is the fact that God trusted them with His law. He had dwelt with His people. His presence had been in the Holy of Holies in the temple. Violence and the worship of a false god go together. It appears they have purposely angered God. God wants Ezekiel to understand why He has judged these people harshly.

Ezekiel 8:18 "Therefore will I also deal in fury: mine eye shall not spare, neither will I have pity: and though they cry in mine ears with a loud voice, will I not hear them."

They had boldly denounced their love for God by worshiping these false gods. Israel was His loving wife. She had gone away to the love of false gods. Israel had committed spiritual adultery. She had not only done this terrible thing but had openly done it in full view of God. God will now punish her in full view of the world around her. He will take justified vengeance upon her with no pity. They may cry out to God, but He will not listen. It is too late.

CHAPTERS 12

Woe to Foolish Prophets

Ezekiel Chapter 13

Ezekiel 13:1 "And the word of the LORD came unto me, saying, "The Word of the Lord is to the people's prophets, and not to the entire nation. Ezekiel 13:2 "Son of man, prophesy against the prophets of Israel that prophesy, and say thou unto them that prophesy out of their hearts, Hear ye the word of the Lord;."

This prophecy is directed to the false prophets only. These prophets should not be ministering to anyone because they do not even know the truth themselves. False prophets had long flourished in Judah and were transported to Babylon. Here God directs Ezekiel to indict those false prophets for fruitless assurances of peace. Then His attention turns to lying prophetesses (in verses 17-23).

Those who would be teachers then, or now, must first learn themselves. Many called in the ministry, but they did not prepare. The most extraordinary preparation a man can make is thoroughly studying God's Word. The Truth is in the Word of God. A person should never go into the ministry as a profession. The ministry must be a call.

In the case of the true prophets, their mouths are not their own. God speaks to the people through them. The words are not from the prophets' hearts but the heart of God. The false prophets in Israel were not unintentionally in error. They had made up these prophecies themselves, pretending the message came from God.

Ezekiel 13:3 "Thus saith the Lord God; Woe unto the foolish prophets, that follow their spirit, and have seen nothing!"

Woe introduces a curse on false prophets. They were like the working man who tried to cover a cracked wall with whitewash.

It is perilous for a person to pretend to hear from God when he is not. Only a very foolish person would do it. The punishment for this would come from God and not from man. Sometimes a person would claim to be a prophet to be recognized. A true prophet does not have an easy life. We can look at Jeremiah, Isaiah, Daniel, and Ezekiel and see they are not showered with good times. They mostly have a tough time. Sometimes their own families do not even believe them.

Ezekiel 13:4 "O Israel, thy prophets are like the desert foxes."

Foxes are clever and tricky. These false prophets are harsh too. They were not telling the truth. They were telling things to make them look good and be respected in the community. They appeal to the flesh of man.

A prophet of God brings warnings to the people. Seldom are they proclaiming beautiful times for the present? The ultimate way to tell who is a false or a true prophet is, did their prophecy come true?

Ezekiel 13:5 "Ye have not gone up into the gaps, neither made up the hedge for the house of Israel to stand in the battle in the day of the Lord."

They should have been calling their people to repentance. Instead, they were betraying their people with these false prophecies. They were not standing in the gap. They were trying to benefit themselves, not the people.

Ezekiel 13:6 "They have seen arrogance and lying divination, saying, The Lord said: and the Lord has not sent them: and they have made others hope that they would confirm the word."

True prophets used the statement "Thus said the Lord." False prophets were using The Lord said statements without being sent of the Lord. It appears they were not only deceiving others but themselves.

The arrogance speaks of them serving themselves. Divination, in this instance, is telling of witchcraft. Their messages were coming from Satan.

Ezekiel 13:7 "Have ye not seen a vain vision, and have ye not spoken a lying divination, whereas ye say, The Lord saith, I have not spoken?"

These false prophets have deliberately tried to injure the good name of the Lord. The people may not realize that this message is not from God, but God and the false prophets know. God tells them through Ezekiel here that they are not deceiving Him.

Ezekiel 13:8 "Therefore thus saith the Lord GOD; Because ye have spoken vanity, and seen lies, therefore, behold, I am against you, saith the Lord GOD."

This is a strong statement that fits the false prophets of old and the false prophets of our day, as well. God never changes. He is against the false prophets today also. We must be careful in our prophecy not to prophesy things for our benefit. God loves Truth.

Ezekiel 13:9 "And my hand shall be upon the prophets that see vanity, and that divine lies: they shall not be in the assembly of my people, neither shall they be written in the writing of the house of Israel, neither shall they enter into the land of Israel; and ye shall know that I am the Lord GOD."

There is a three-fold judgment given to the false prophets:

- ❖ They would not be in the counsel of God's people.
- ❖ Their names would be wiped from the register of Israel; and

❖   They would never return to the land.

This is saying that God will stop them from prophesying, and their name will be taken off the role. Israel was well known for its record-keeping, but they will not be those records. They will not be included when Israel is restored. It is speaking of a curse that comes upon them, and they will not be remembered. They will not even be citizens anymore. God, Himself, makes them outcasts.

Ezekiel 13:10 "Because, even because they have seduced my people, saying, Peace; and there was no peace, and one built up a wall, and, lo, others daubed it with un-tempered mortar.

Their work had been in vain. They had built with things that would not withstand time of trouble. They had been speaking of peace, and there was no peace. They were leading others to destruction, while all the time, they were pretending they were building them up.

False prophets had lulled the people into false security. False "peace" promises, while sin continued on the brink of God's judgment, were a way to erect a defective "wall" and whitewash it to make it look good. An unsafe "wall" was doomed to collapse when God would bring His storm, picturing the invader's assault.

Ezekiel 13:11 "Say unto them which smeared it with un-tempered mortar, that it shall fall there shall be an overflowing shower; and ye, O great hailstones, shall fall; and a stormy wind shall tear it."

It is like the house built upon the sand that could not stand when the rains of life came. This wall, the same as the house of sand, had no solid foundation. The wind, the rain, or the hailstones could destroy this faulty building. Their prophecies could not withstand times of trouble either. Of course, all these descriptions are images belonging to the illustration of the wall, not meant to convey natural wind, flood, and hail. The Babylonians were the actual destroyers of Israel's hypocritical false spirituality.

Ezekiel 13:12 "Lo, when the wall is fallen, shall it not be said unto you, where is the smear wherewith ye have smeared it?"

It speaks of their prophecy, which was supposed to happen right away. When the time comes and does not occur, they will be declared false prophets. All their predictions were wasted. Their prophecies did not help anyone, not even themselves.

Ezekiel 13:13 "Therefore thus saith the Lord GOD; I will even tear it with a stormy wind in my fury, and there shall be an overflowing shower in mine anger, and great hailstones in my fury to consume it."

God is speaking through Ezekiel to these false prophets. God's fury will be destroyed, and the false prophets will be consumed.

Ezekiel 13:14 "So will I break down the wall that ye have smeared with un-tempered mortar, and bring it down to the ground so that the foundation thereof shall be discovered, and it shall fall, and ye shall be consumed in the midst thereof: and ye shall know that I am the Lord."

This wall of false prophecy smeared it to make it stand; it will not stand. The fury of God will bring it down and will also destroy these false prophets. There will be no question that this is God's fury on the false prophets. The only wall that will stand in the time of trouble is the wall that is built on a solid foundation. The Lord must be the Cornerstone. We make with truth; any other wall will fall.

Ezekiel 13:15 "Thus will I accomplish my wrath upon the wall, and them that have smeared it with un-tempered mortar, and will say unto you, the wall is no more, neither they that smear it."

The physical wall around Jerusalem will come down. All the prophecies of better times, which are not from God, will not keep the wall from coming down. When there was no peace, those who gave these prophecies of peace gave people false hope. The false prophet will be destroyed along with the warning he gave.

Ezekiel 13:16 The prophets of Israel which prophecy concerning Jerusalem, and see visions of peace for her, and there is no peace, saith the Lord God."

It is an exacting statement, telling exactly who these false prophets are and what they're teaching the people.

Ezekiel 13:17 "Likewise, thou son of man, set thy face against the daughters of thy people, which prophecy out of their own heart; and prophesy thou against them,"

Women have had a significant influence on the religion of their country from the very beginning. Some of them have been to honor, and some to dishonor. It quickly suggests the women who were crying over the false god in: Ezekiel 8:14 "Then he brought me to the door of the gate of the LORD'S house which was toward the north; and behold, there sat women weeping for Tammuz."

The women are false prophetesses. They are like false prophets and will suffer the same condemnation.

Ezekiel 13:18 "And say, thus saith the Lord GOD; Woe to the women that sew pillows to all armholes and make kerchiefs upon the head of every stature to hunt souls! Will ye hunt the souls of my people, and will ye save the souls alive [that come] unto you?"

The pillows sewn to the armholes have been interpreted to refer to either amulet placed upon the wrists that supposedly communicated magical powers to the enchanter or bonds tied around the wrists of the enquirer that symbolized magically that the associated spell or incantation was a binding one. These sorceresses utilized all these things in their divinations, hunting down souls for their advantage (verse 20).

Ezekiel 13:19 "And will ye pollute me among my people for handfuls of barley and pieces of bread, slay the souls that should not die, and save the souls alive that should not live, by your lying to my people that hear your lies?"

Whatever they were doing, they charged for it. It was like fortune-telling, perhaps. We know that there was very sensual worship going on at this time, so it could have been that.

Ezekiel 13:20 "Wherefore thus saith the Lord GOD; Behold, I am against your pillows, wherewith ye there hunt the souls to make them fly, and I will tear them from your arms and will let the souls go, even the souls that ye hunt to make them fly."

These pillows probably had some writing upon them. They were more likely used in fortune-telling. They had amulets with writing upon them. This pillow has something to do with snaring the people like a bird in a net. It is unimportant what the evil was. It is enough to know that they are stealing souls away from God to false gods. It is incredibly evil.

Ezekiel 13:21 "Your kerchiefs also will I tear, and deliver my people out of your hand, and they shall be no more in your hand to be hunted, and ye shall know that I am the Lord."

It seems they have some spell over the people as if they were bonded. God will free the people from these evil women.

Ezekiel 13:22 "Because with lies ye have made the heart of the righteous sad, whom I have not made sad; and strengthened the hands of the wicked, that he should not return from his wicked way, by promising him life:"

They have not offered hope to the righteous. They have saddened them. They were on the side of the wicked. Ezekiel and Jeremiah had preached repentance and hope for the righteous. These false prophetesses have taught the opposite. Predators had saddened the righteous with a wrong message leading to a calamity that involved significant loss.

They had encouraged the wicked to expect a bright future and saw no need to repent to avoid death.

Ezekiel 13:23 "Therefore ye shall see no more vanity, nor divine divinations: for I will deliver my people out of your hand: and ye shall know that I am the Lord."

Divination had to do with witchcraft. God is the only one who can free a person from the grip of witchcraft. God would have to deliver them. There is no power on this earth that is not subject to God. When God speaks, every knee bows. I will provide for my people: Certainly, this was true in the restoration after the seventy years in Babylon but will be entirely true in Messiah's coming kingdom. God's faithful promise will bring an end to sorcery and false prophecy.

CHAPTER 13

Idolatry will be Punished

Ezekiel 14: 1-11

Ezekiel 14:1 "Then came certain of the elders of Israel unto me and sat before me." It is the beginning of a new prophecy. These elders were those who had been trained in the Word of God. They have heard the other predictions and are inquiring of Ezekiel about themselves.

These leaders came insincerely seeking God's counsel, as God revealed to the prophet, who thus saw through their facade and indicted them for determining to pursue their evil way and defy God's will. They had set up their idols in their hearts. Their idolatry, unlike that back in Jerusalem, was internal.

Ezekiel 14:2 "And the word of the Lord came unto me, saying," One thing that we could take advice from is that Ezekiel speaks just what God puts in His mouth.

Ezekiel 14:3 "Son of man, these men have set up their idols in their heart, and put the stumbling block of their iniquity before their face: should I be enquired of at all by them?"

The heart reveals what we are. It is the center of our being. Man is either lost or saved by what is in his heart. Even though the idols have been burned, they still think of them with fond memories. God is saying if they still have these idols in their hearts, why do not they consult them, and not Me? An idol does not have to be one you can see with your eyes. Anything, or anyone, that you put above God in your heart is an idol. Their hearts have not stayed upon God.

Ezekiel 14:4 "Therefore speak unto them, and say unto them, Thus saith the Lord GOD; every man of the house of Israel that set up his idols in his heart, and put the stumbling block of his iniquity before his face, and cometh to the prophet; I the LORD will answer him that cometh according to the multitude of his idols;."

Sin does not have to be physically carried out to be sin. The heart of man will be judged. Jesus said in Matthew:

Matthew 5:28 "But I say unto you, that whosoever look on a woman to lust after her hath committed adultery with her already in his heart."

These elders have sinned in their hearts because they still worship idols. True worship takes place in the heart. To replace worship of God with idols is to separate oneself from God. Even thinking of worshipping God while we still have thoughts of idols in our hearts is impossible as well. God will not share His people with anyone or anything else. You cannot worship God and idols at the same time. They received no verbal answer but directly from the Lord in the action of judgment.

Ezekiel 14:5 "That I may take the house of Israel in their own heart because they are all estranged from me through their idols."

Their idolatry had brought this captivity upon them. "Estranged," in this verse, means to be a foreigner or turn aside. They have turned away from God in their hearts. The double-minded person is not acceptable to God.

Ezekiel 14:6 "Therefore say unto the house of Israel, Thus saith the Lord GOD; Repent, and turn yourselves from your idols, and turn away your faces from all your abominations."

It is speaking to all the people, including these elders. **Notice:** This is to the entire house of Israel, not just these elders.

Look at the word "yourselves. The Lord answered the two-faced inquiry in only one way, by a call to repent. The seekers have turned away from Him to idols, and He turned away from them. We see that the decision to worship or not worship God is an individual thing. Each person decides to turn away from his abominations to the Living God in his own heart.

Just as John the Baptist preached to repent, the message is also here. God will forgive. The individual must repent, and then God will come and dwell with him again.

Ezekiel 14:7 "For every one of the houses of Israel, or of the stranger that sojourned in Israel, which separated himself from me, and set up his idols in his heart, and put the stumbling block of his iniquity before his face, and cometh to a prophet to enquire of him concerning me; I the LORD will answer him by myself:"\

"Everyone" leaves no doubt that this is an individual thing. Notice that this is not just the Hebrews but the strangers as well. Another word for a stranger would be Gentile. "Sojourned" means temporarily dwells. Those who purposely turn from God to idols will someday stand before the Judge of all the world and be found guilty. God deals with this Himself. It does not have to be an open act of idolatry. The heart is judged.

We see Jesus speaking of this very thing in the following Scripture on judgment day. Matthew 7:22-23 "Many will say to me in that day, Lord, have we not prophesied in thy name? and in thy name have cast out devils? and in thy name done many wonderful works?" "And then will I profess unto them, I never knew you: depart from me, ye that work iniquity."

Their outward action was alright, but God judges the heart. Their hearts were not acceptable.

Ezekiel 14:8 "And I will set my face against that man and make him a sign and a proverb, and I will cut him off from the midst of my people, and ye shall know that I am the Lord."

God is not interested in our outward show of faith. He judges the heart. God will turn His face from one who does not retain Him in his heart. That man will be thought of God and used to show others the error of this. Only God knows the heart of man. There will be no question, and this judgment is of God.

Ezekiel 14:9 "And if the prophet is deceived when he hath spoken a thing, I the LORD have deceived that prophet, and I will stretch out my hand upon him and destroy him from the midst of my people Israel."

There were false prophets in the land. God had judged their hearts and found them guilty of worshipping idols in their hearts. God causes them to believe a lie because they are not faithful to Him. God builds up whoever He will, and He destroys whoever He will. His judgment is just. _God removes prophets, as it is God who builds up prophets._

God will let a prophet be deceived, and that false prophet will only be in a trained sense. When one willfully rejects His Word, He places a resulting cloud of darkness or allows it to continue, hiding the truth so that the person is deceived by his obstinate self-will.

It fits with the same principle as when God gives up Israel to evil statutes, counsel they insist on as they reject His Word. When people refuse the truth, He lets them seek after their feelings and gives them over to falsehood. It is the wrath of abandonment (Romans 1:18).

Ezekiel 14:10 "And they shall bear the punishment of their iniquity: the punishment of the prophet shall be even as the punishment of him that seek unto him;."

There is a responsibility for those listening to prophets to determine whether they are of God. To follow a false prophet brings the follower the same punishment as the false prophet.

1 John 4:1 "Beloved, believe not every spirit, but try the spirits whether they are of God: because many false prophets are gone out into the world."

Ezekiel 14:11 "That the house of Israel may go no more astray from me, neither be polluted any more with all their transgressions; but that they may be my people, and I may be their God, saith the Lord GOD."

Every punishment that God brings on this earth is to cause those living in sin to repent. God desires to be their God. He will not force Himself upon them. They must choose to be His people, and then He will be their God.

CHAPTER 14

Judgment on Persistent Unfaithfulness

Ezekiel 14: 12-23

Ezekiel 14:12 "The word of the LORD came again to me, saying," another break in the prophecy here.

Ezekiel 14:13 "Son of man, when the land sin against me by trespassing terribly, then will I stretch out my hand upon it, and will break the staff of the bread thereof, and will send famine upon it, and will cut off man and beast from it:"

God is speaking to Ezekiel here. Son of man is a name by which God calls Ezekiel. We see that famine is one way that God brings punishment to an unrepentant society. Much of the famine in our community today is in areas where they worship false gods or no God

Ezekiel 14:14 "Though these three men, Noah, Daniel, and Job, were in it, they should deliver but their souls by their righteousness, saith the Lord God."

God spoke of the three mentioned above as being righteous in His sight. They lived in a society that was far away from God. The situation in Judah is so desperate that even if three of the most righteous men in the history of God's people were to intercede, they would be able to save only themselves. Noah preached to the people around him the many years he was building the ark, but no one listened and repented. God saved Noah, his wife, his three sons, and their three wives. Noah was not protected from the flood; he was kept in flood. Daniel was saved in the lion's den, not from it. Job was held in the presence of his friends who did not believe. God may not remove you from your problem, but He will protect you in the difficulty if you stay in the right standing with Him.

This scripture demonstrates that even the presence and prayers of the godly could not stop the coming judgment. (Genesis 18:22-32 and Jer. 5:1-4), provides rare exceptions to the principle that one man's righteousness is no protection for others.

Ezekiel 14:15 "If I cause horrible beasts to pass through the land, and they spoil it, so that it be desolate, that no man may pass through because of the beasts:"

The noisome beasts would be for the punishment of those living in sin. The problem will be there, but God will protect His own amid the situation. Remember the one who held the inkhorn and the other five angels who were to mark certain ones.

Ezekiel 14:16" Though these three men were in it, as I live, saith the Lord GOD, they shall deliver neither sons nor daughters; they only shall be provided, but the land shall be desolate."

It explains our originality of salvation. Just because you are righteous in God's sight does not mean your children are. God judges on an individual basis. You repent and live for God to save your soul. The land is desolate in punishment for sin. God will protect His own, even in a famine.

Ezekiel 14:17 "Or I bring a sword upon that land, and say, Sword, go through the land; so that I cut off man and beast from it:"

It is another form of punishment that God brings upon those who have turned against Him. Those who genuinely love God may be in the land when these problems come, but the sword will not kill them. A thousand may fall at their side, but God will protect them.

Ezekiel 14:18 "Though these three men were in it, as I live, saith the Lord GOD, they shall deliver neither sons nor daughters, but they only shall be delivered themselves."

It is just saying that God does not have grandchildren, just children. These sons, and daughters, must decide for themselves to follow God. Each generation is judged on its own merits.

Ezekiel 14:19 "I send a pestilence into that land, and pour out my fury upon it in blood, to cut off from man and beast:"

Again, this is speaking of a different type of judgment that might come into the land because of the sin. It is not from Satan. It is from God, against a rebellious family.

Ezekiel 14:20 "Though Noah, Daniel, and Job were in it, as I live, saith the Lord God, they shall deliver neither son nor daughter; they shall but deliver their souls by their righteousness."

Noah, Daniel, and Job were three righteous men who lived in the same land with very few people. Just explains, again, that their righteousness would not save their children. Only the children's righteousness could keep them. Each person is responsible for their sin.

Three people come to mind here, Seth, Ham, and Japheth.

Genesis 9:18 "And the sons of Noah, that went forth of the ark, were Shem, and Ham, and Japheth: and Ham is the father of Canaan."

Genesis 10:6 "And the sons of Ham; Cush, Miriam, Phut, and Canaan."

Both Cush and Phut are mentioned as significant players in the end-time prophecies as those who will come against Israel.

Ezekiel 14:21 "For thus saith the Lord God; How much more when I send my four sore judgments upon Jerusalem, the sword, the famine, the noisome beast, and the pestilence, to cut off from it man and beast?"

God sends these four judgments upon all the people who have committed spiritual adultery in their hearts by worshiping false gods.

The chastisement of God is excellent in these four judgments, but the sin was just as great. God fits the punishment for the wrong.

Ezekiel 14:22 "Yet, behold, therein shall be left a remnant that shall be brought forth, sons and daughters: behold, they shall come forth unto you, and ye shall see their way and their doings: and ye shall be comforted concerning the evil that I have brought upon Jerusalem, concerning all that I have brought upon it."

God always saved a remnant of His people. These are they who have not bowed their knees to false gods. The beautiful thing in all of this is that God does not group everyone. Those who live for Him will be saved, even though everyone around them is lost. God never overlooks a single person who loves Him.

In 1 Corinthians 8:3, "But if any man loves God, the same is known of him." God's judgment on Jerusalem was just. His saving of the remnant was just as well.

Ezekiel 14:23 "And they shall comfort you when ye see their ways and their doings: and ye shall know that I have not done without cause all that I have done in it, saith the Lord God."

The comfort is in the knowledge of the remnant saved, who will return to Jerusalem later. There has been a separation of evil from good in the judgments of God. God is loving and kind, but He is also just. His cause was holy, and therefore we do not always understand.

An ungodly Jerusalem remnant, brought as captives to join exiled Jews in Babylon, was very wicked. Exiles already there, repulsed by this evil, were to realize God's justness in His severe judgment on Jerusalem.

CHAPTER 15

The Broken Covenant

Jeremiah 11:1-17

Jeremiah 11:1 "The word that came to Jeremiah from the Lord," Jeremiah's messages reveal Judah's false loyalties. They have been unfaithful to the covenant of the LORD and, accordingly, must suffer the consequences of their infidelity. Judah's corruption had led them to an excessive pride that resulted in them suffering humiliation.

Jeremiah 11:2 "Hear ye the words of this covenant, and speak unto the men of Judah and the inhabitants of Jerusalem;"

"The covenant": This is to God's covenant, summarized in which promised curses for disobeying and blessings for obeying (Deut. 27:26 – 28:68).

To read a more detailed account of the covenant spoken of, read all (2 Kings Chapter 23). This also goes into detail about the sins of the people. Jeremiah is to first hear from God and then speak to the men of Jerusalem. This was not communicated to just those who held high positions but to all the inhabitants.

Jeremiah 11:3 "And say thou unto them, thus saith the LORD God of Israel; Cursed [be] the man that obeys not the words of this covenant,"

It shows that the command of dispensing the law or covenant was principally given to Jeremiah. "Thus, saith the Lord God of Israel": That made them, brought them out of Egypt, and made a covenant with them. And had taken care of them and had bestowed many favors upon them. "Cursed be the man that obeys not the words of this covenant": Which the prophet, it may be, had in his hands, even the book of the law; and held it forth unto them, while he was speaking.

The language of which is: cursed is everyone who does not constantly and perfectly perform what is contained (Deut. 27:26). God had promised the land of milk and honey to those who kept a covenant with Him. He also promised that those who broke the covenant would be cursed. One of the most important things about the covenant was to keep the Passover. It was a requirement.

Jeremiah 11:4 "Which I commanded your fathers in the day I brought them forth out of the land of Egypt, from the iron furnace, saying, obey my voice, and do them, according to all which I command you: so, shall ye be my people, and I will be your God:"

"The iron furnace": A metaphor for the hardship of Egyptian bondage hundreds of years earlier (Exodus 1:8-14).

The Passover was something they were to keep as long as they were alive. The Passover celebrated the night when death passed over the Hebrew houses that had the blood of the Lamb over the door. It was the very thing that caused Pharaoh to release them. They had been enslaved people in Egypt. Egypt kept them under hard bondage.

It was the birth of the Israelite nation. God promised to be their God if they kept His commandments.

Jeremiah 11:5 "That I may perform the oath which I have sworn unto your fathers, to give them a land flowing with milk and honey, as this day. Then answered I and said, so be it, O Lord." Your fathers" Abraham, Isaac, and Jacob. "To give them a land flowing with milk and honey": That is, abounding with plenty of provisions (Exodus 3:8).

"As it is this day": The land of Canaan continued to be, in those times, a very fruitful country. It was as it was promised it would be, and there was no doubt about it; Their eyes saw it, and the day bore witness to it. "Then answered I, and said": That is, the Prophet Jeremiah, to whom the above order was given. "So be it, O Lord": Or "Amen, Lord ": Either deciding to publish what the Lord commanded him or wishing that the land of Canaan might continue to be the same fruitful land it was.

And the Jewish people in it, keeping the words of this covenant. Or else, as agreeing that the curse might fall upon the men that did not observe them (Deut. 27:15). God still wanted them to have the land of milk and honey, but they must keep their part of the bargain. "So be it" and "Amen" express the same thing. Jeremiah agrees with everything God has said.

Jeremiah 11:6 "Then the LORD said unto me, proclaim all these words in the cities of Judah, and the streets of Jerusalem, saying, "Hear ye the words of this covenant and do them."

"Proclaim all these words in the cities of Judah, and in the streets of Jerusalem": With a loud voice, and openly, that all may hear.

"Saying, hear ye the words of this covenant, and do them,": Which their forefathers promised when the covenant was made with them (Exodus 24:7) but did not perform. Hearing without doing is of little avail. Not the hearers, but the doers of the law are justified; wherefore, men should not be content with hearing only (Rom. 2:13).

Jeremiah was to reread the covenant to the people of Judah and in Jerusalem. It is the last warning for them to keep their covenant with God. Jeremiah 11:7 "For I earnestly protested unto your fathers in the day I brought them up out of the land of Egypt, unto this day, rising early and protesting, saying, Obey my voice. "Or "witnessing, witnessed"; testified His great affection for them. Persistently solicited their observation of His precepts for their good. And strictly cautioned them against neglect and disobedience. "The day that I brought them out of the land of Egypt": (Jer.11:4)."Even unto this day rising early and protesting, saying, obey my voice": That is, from the time of the giving of the law, in all successive ages, to the present time. He had sent His prophets to them, time after time, morning by morning, early and late, to press, encourage, and stir them up to obedience to His will. And to warn them of the evils that would come by disobedience. The message from God had never changed. He wanted them to obey His commands.

Their fathers, freed from Egypt, wandered in the wilderness for forty years because of their disobedience. It seems these people never learn. God would protect them and provide for all their needs if they would just obey Him.

Jeremiah 11:8 "Yet they obeyed not, nor inclined their ear, but walked everyone in the imagination of their evil heart: therefore, I will bring upon them all the words of this covenant, which I commanded [them] to do; but they did them not."

Though they had such solid solicitations and fair warnings, repeated and repeated. Then an annoyance of their disobedience and stubbornness.

"But walked everyone in the imagination of their evil heart": Which is desperately wicked, and is evil, and that continually; even every imagination of it. Wherefore walking herein must be very gratifying to the flesh and different from walking in the law of the Lord and obeying it (Jer. 3:17).

"Therefore, I will bring upon them all the words of this covenant": All the curses and threats mentioned in it against the disobedient. And so, the Targum says, "and I brought upon them vengeance or punishment because they received not the words of this covenant:"

"Which I commanded them to do; but they did them not": Because they did not do the law's commands, therefore the curses of it lighted on them. For the words of the preceding clause may be rendered, "and I brought upon them." And it is advised that the punishment would be inflicted on the present generation as they are imitating and pursuing the iniquities of their fathers. Since they did not obey, they could expect the curses instead of the blessings. Again, these are spelled out in (Deut. 28:15-68).

Deuteronomy 28:45-46 "Moreover all these curses shall come upon thee, and shall pursue thee, and overtake thee, till thou be destroyed; because thou hearken not unto the voice of the Lord thy God, to keep his commandments and his statutes which he commanded thee:"

"And they shall be upon you for a sign and wonder and upon your seed forever." Verses 9-10: The people repeated their forefathers' errors so closely that God called their behavior a "conspiracy." Every generation has the chance to live under the covenant or break it. Meanwhile, God remains faithful to His character and His word (2 Tim. 2:13).

Jeremiah 11:9 "And the LORD said unto me, A conspiracy is found among the men of Judah and the inhabitants of Jerusalem."

"A conspiracy": The deliberate resisting of God's appeals for repentance and an insistence upon trusting their own "peace" message and idols. The conspiracy was against God. The plot is just speaking that both Judah and Jerusalem had broken their covenant with God.

Jeremiah 11:10 "They are turned back to the iniquities of their forefathers, which refused to hear my words; and they went after other gods to serve them: the house of Israel and the house of Judah have broken my covenant which I made with their fathers."

According to Kimchi, this prophecy was delivered in the times of Jehoiakim. There had been a reforming during the reign of Josiah, but now they had rebelled against the Lord and had returned to their former idolatries that had been practiced in the times of Amon, Manasseh, and Ahaz. "Which refused to hear my words": Sent unto them by the prophets, Isaiah, and others. "And they went after other gods to serve them": Not their forefathers, though it was true of them; but the then-present generation in the conspiracy and rebellion against God. They put their schemes into execution and worshiped and served the nations' gods.

"The house of Israel and the house of Judah have broken my covenant which I made with their fathers": By their many transgressions, and especially by their idolatry; the house of Israel, or the ten tribes, had done so, many years ago, and were carried captive. And the house of Judah, or the two tribes of Benjamin and Judah, committing the same iniquities, might justly expect the like treatment.

The iniquities of their forefathers were their purpose of worshiping and serving false gods. It seems that time had not caused their unfaithfulness to go away. They were committing the same sins their forefathers and fathers committed. The main thing to remember is that God did not break the covenant He made; Israel and Judah did. Verses 11-13: Although calamity might make the people "cry unto me," "God," they would quickly revert to their pattern and seek other "gods" who "shall not save them at all." God knows fake faith and false repentance, no matter what it looks or sounds like.

Jeremiah 11:11 "Therefore thus saith the LORD, Behold, I will bring evil upon them, which they shall not be able to escape; and though they shall cry unto me, I will not hearken unto them."

God's deafness to Judah's "cry" was sufficient evidence of their sin. Not only had Judah broken God's covenant, but they had gone off into a corrupt lifestyle of paganism. Therefore, their fellowship with

God was broken, and He would not hear their requests (Psalm 68:18; John 9:31; James 4:3).

Where there is godless living (Isa. 56:11-12), lack of concern for others in their need (Isa. 58:6-9), and carelessness regarding the explicit instructions of the Word of God (35:17), God cannot honor the one who prays. Instead, such a one stands in danger of divine judgment (Zech. 7:8-14). However, where the intimacy of communion exists, God answers His own call (Job 13:22; 14:14-15; Psalms 22:24-25; 91:15; 102:1-2; Isa. 58:9; 65:24).

"Therefore" is the keyword in this. It connects with the preceding verse, which tells of the breaking of the covenant. The Scripture here is just explaining the results of their broken covenant. Their deliberate unfaithfulness to God will bring evil upon them. The sad thing in all of this is that God will no longer hear their prayers. It is the effectual fervent prayer of a righteous man that availed much. The best way to get prayers answered is to be right-standing with God.

Jeremiah 11:12 "Then shall the cities of Judah and inhabitants of Jerusalem go, and cry unto the gods unto whom they offer incense: but they shall not save them at all in the time of their trouble."

The inhabitants of the cities of Judah and the inhabitants of the city of Jerusalem, the former being in distress on account of the enemy plundering and destroying their land, after the latter had been besieged and taken captive. Go and cry unto the gods unto whom they offer incense": Baal, the queen of heaven, and the sun, moon, planets, and all the hosts of heaven, as in (Jer. 44:15). These they should cry unto for help and deliverance in vain. But they shall not save them at all in the time of their trouble": Not yield them the minor relief or comfort in their situation, so far from protecting them entirely from it. Since God will not listen to their prayers, they go and pray to these false gods. That is the very thing that got them in trouble with God in the first place. The idol has no power at all to help anyone. Their prayers then were futile.

Jeremiah 11:13 "For the number of thy cities were thy gods, O Judah; and the number of the streets of Jerusalem have ye set up altars to the shameful thing, altars to burn incense unto Baal."

Judah was so filled with idolatry that there were false deities for every city and a polluted altar on every street.

Baal was the name of one of the false gods. It appears they worshipped many false gods. King Manasseh had raised numerous altars to false gods.

Jeremiah 11:14 "Therefore pray not thou for this people, neither lift a cry or prayer for them: for I will not hear when they cry unto me for their trouble."

"Pray not thou for this people": If they rejected God, their prayers could not gain the answers they desired (Psalm 66:18).

These people have placed their faith in false gods, so God tells Jeremiah not to pray to Him for them. He is saying, let their false gods help them. God's anger against their unfaithfulness is excellent. God will not allow them this time. Verses 15-17: One of God's nicknames for His people was "Green Olive Tree," a picture of health and blessing. And yet the people's sins had dried up the branches and made them as kindling.

Jeremiah 11:15 "What hath my beloved to do in mine house, seeing she hath wrought lewdness with many, and the holy flesh is passed from thee? when thou do evil, then thou rejoice."

"My beloved": A phrase showing God's sensitive regard for His relationship to Israel as a nation. However, it does not carry the assumption that every individual is spiritually saved.

"**Wrought lewdness** with many": Shameful idolatry that defiled all that befits true temple worship (Ezek. 8:6-13). These were gross violations of the first three commandments (Exodus 20:2-7).

"Holy flesh": In some way, they corrupted the animal sacrifices by committing sin, which they enjoyed.

The family of Israel, including Benjamin and Judah, was spoken of as God's wife. For them to follow false gods is the same thing as committing spiritual adultery. They were God's beloved, but they have left Him.

Verses 16-17 "Green olive tree": Israel was pictured as a grapevine, then an olive tree meant to bear good fruit. However, they produced fruit that calls only for the fire of judgment.

Jeremiah 11:16 "The LORD called thy name, A green olive tree, fair, of goodly fruit: with the noise of a great tumult, he hath kindled fire upon it, and its branches are broken."

The Jewish church and people to one and made them one. Very prosperous and flourishing in the enjoyment of privileges, civil and religious and being highly favored with the word and ordinances.

"Fair, and of goodly fruit": for a while, brought forth the fruit of good works and was cheerful and goodly to look upon; was, as the Syriac version says, "fair with fruit, and beautiful insight." And whereas it might have been expected she would have so continued and been still as a green olive tree in the house of God, as David says in Psalm 52:8. Now it was; otherwise, she became barren, dry, and fruitless; and therefore, it follows:

"With the noise of a great tumult He hath kindled fire upon it": Utilizing the Chaldean army, which came with a mighty rushing noise. The Lord hath destroyed Judah and burnt it with fire. What the Chaldeans did is ascribed to God because it was done according to His will and by His direction and overruling providence. And the branches of it are broken": The high and principal ones, the king, princes, and nobles, their palaces, and the house of God. The apostle seems to have respect for this passage in (Rom. 11:17). The Targum says, "as an olive tree that is beautiful in form and comely of sight, whose branches overshadow the trees, so the LORD hath magnified thy name among the people. But now that thou hast transgressed the law, the armies of the people, who are strong as fire, shall come against you, and others shall join them. Some of the olive trees in Israel are thought to have lived thousands of years. They are of hardy stock. The green olive tree would have many years to produce fruit. The righteous man is, many times, spoken of as the green olive tree. They would have been God's forever had they not strayed.

Now God has broken off the branches and will burn them. They are no more beautiful to God. There will, however, be a remnant left. The stock will spring forth new branches.

Jeremiah 11:17 "For the LORD of hosts, that planted thee, hath pronounced evil against thee, for the evil of the house of Israel and of the house of Judah, which they have done against themselves to provoke me to anger in offering incense unto Baal."

Like a green olive tree, and gave thee all thy freshness, fruitfulness, happiness, and prosperity; when He first put thee into the possession of the good land and recognized thee by so many favors and blessings. As He can take them away, so He will.

"For He hath pronounced evil against you ": He has determined it in His mind, and He has declared it by His prophets. For the evil of the house of Israel": The ten tribes had sinned, for which the evil pronounced had been executed on them already, as they were captive sometime earlier.

"And of the house of Judah": Who had taken no warning but had followed them in their iniquities and exceeded them. And therefore, they must expect punishment for their sins.

"Which they have done against themselves": For sin is not only against God, His nature, will, and law; but it is against the sinner himself. And is to his hurt and ruin, both earthly and eternal.

"To provoke me to anger in offering incense unto Baal": This mainly was the evil which was so provoking to God. And therefore, He determined to bring the evil of punishment upon them; and shows the cause and reason of it; and which is a sufficient vindication of His justice.

This is very similar to the fig tree that Jesus cursed because it did not produce fruit. God planted the olive tree that symbolizes Israel. He also planted the fig tree, which symbolizes Israel. Sin cursed them. They had brought the evil upon themselves. When incense was burned to God, it represented the prayers to God. This incense burned to Baal showed they were putting their faith and trust in this false god, Baal.

CHAPTER 16

Trusting In Lying Lips

Jeremiah 7:1-17

Jeremiah 7:1 "The word that came to Jeremiah from the LORD, saying," "The word that came": This was Jeremiah's first temple sermon. God was aroused against the sins He named, especially at His temple, becoming a "den of robbers."

However, the point of this message was that if Israel repented, even at this late hour, God would keep the conqueror from coming. They must reject lies such as the false hope that peace is confident, based on the reasoning that the Lord would never bring calamity to His temple. They must turn from their sins and end their hypocrisy.

Jeremiah 7:2 "Stand in the gate of the Lord's house, proclaim this word, and say, Hear the word of the Lord, all you of Judah, that enter in at these gates to worship the Lord."

That is, of the temple and the court of it. This gate, as Kimchi says, was the eastern gate, which was the principal gate of all (Jer. 26:2). "And proclaim there this word, and say": With a loud voice, as follows:

"Hear ye the word of the Lord, all ye of Judah": The inhabitants of the several parts of Judea came to the temple to worship. It was probably a feast day, neither the Passover, Pentecost, or feast of tabernacles, when all the males in Israel appeared in court.

"That enter in at these gates to worship the Lord": Seven gates were belonging to the court, three on the north, three on the south, and one in the east, the chief of all, as Kimchi, Abarbanel, and Ben Melech observe; and the account in the Mishna. And therefore, Jeremiah was ordered to stand here and deliver his message.

The first noticeable thing here is that this message is to God's people, not the world. Jeremiah was to go to the house of God and tell God's people. This is spoken to the home of Judah. Notice, "all ye of Judah." The time that Jeremiah was to bring this was a time when large numbers of those of Judah would come to the temple. It is inside the gate. It is a message for God's people alone.

It is a time when pastors should stand on the church's porch and give God's message to the people of God. Notice carefully that Jeremiah was bringing this message from God.

Jeremiah 7:3 "Thus saith the Lord of hosts, the God of Israel, Amend your ways and doings, and I will cause you to dwell in this place."

The Lord of armies above and below in general, and the God of Israel. They ought to hearken to what He was about to say and be obedient to Him.

"Amend your ways and your doings": Or "make them good"; shows that they were terrible and were not agreeable to the law and will of God, to which they ought to have been obeyed. And the way to amend them was to act according to the rule of the divine word they were favored with.

"And I will cause you to dwell in this place": To continue to dwell in Jerusalem and Judea, the land of their nativity, the temple, the house of God, and the place of religious worship. Otherwise, it is indicated that they should not continue here but be carried captive into a strange land.

Jeremiah was crying out to them in the name of the LORD to repent of their evil ways and return to God. God wants to bless them, but He cannot bless them when they worship other gods. He is saying it is not too late if you will repent.

Jeremiah 7:4 "Trust ye not in lying words, saying, the temple of the Lord, the temple of the Lord, the temple of the Lord, these. Jeremiah's God-given message was simple: the natural presence of the "temple" was no guarantee that judgment would not come upon Jerusalem. God's wrath against Judah's sins could be prevented only through genuine repentance that would be reflected in their entire lives.

They are saying over and over, "the temple." They thought if they came to the temple three times a year, that was all that was required. They did not live by their faith in God after leaving the temple. There is more to belonging to God than just attending church occasionally. To be in the right relationship, we must always worship God daily. God has listed four practical and thorough changes to behavior that He expected to see among His people:

- ❖ "Execute judgment thoroughly;
- ❖ Care for "strangers," "the fatherless," and "the widows";
- ❖ "Shed no innocent blood;."
- ❖ Do not pursue "other gods."

God has never lowered His standards; He expects nothing less from His people today.

Jeremiah 7:5 "For if ye thoroughly amend your ways and doings; if ye thoroughly execute judgment between a man and his neighbor;"

The care of the downtrodden and oppressed of society, the "widow," the "orphan," the "poor," and the "stranger," was of particular concern to the God of all mercies. The Book of Deuteronomy recurs elsewhere, too (Job 31:16; Psalms 94:6; 146:9; Isa. 1:17; Jer. 22:3; Ezek. 22:7). This prevalent theme is a vivid reminder for believers to practice righteous standards in their lives and cultivate a social concern for all men like that of God Himself.

Jeremiah 7:6 "If ye oppress not the stranger, the fatherless, and the widow, and shed not innocent blood in this place, neither walk after other gods to your hurt."

Who has none to help them, and who ought to have mercy and compassion shown them and justice done them? And should not be injured by unreasonable sinful men in their persons and properties, and much less oppressed in courts of judgeship by those who should be their supporters and advocates.

"And shed not innocent blood in this place": In the temple, where the Sanhedrin, or great court of judgeship, sat. They do not respect the responsibility of murder by private persons, as the condemnation of innocent men to death by the judges, which is all one as shedding their blood. And by their actions, they defiled that temple where they cried and put their trust. To shed innocent blood in any place, Kimchi observes, is wicked; but to clear it in this place, in the temple, was greater wickedness because this was the place of the Shekinah, or where the divine God dwelt.

"Neither walk after other gods to your hurt": The gods of the people, as the Targum explains; "for this," as the Arabic version renders it, "is destructive to you." Idolatry was more hurtful to themselves than to God; therefore, it is advised against a dispute taken from their interest.

In Jer. 7:5-6, we see that they were not representing God in their day-to-day dealings with the people. They were believers in name only. They lived like the rest of the world. As a ceremony, they came to the temple at the required times. We see a list of the things wrong in their lives in the verses above. God would not accept them as His family until they had a change of heart and lived every day as His ambassadors on the earth. They must turn from the worship of false gods and worship only the true God and treat their neighbors as they would want to be treated.

Jeremiah 7:7 "Then will I cause you to dwell in this place, in the land I gave to your fathers, forever and ever."

"The land that I gave forever": God refers to the unconditional portion of the land promised in the Abrahamic Covenant (Gen. 12, 15, 17, 22). Their being able to live in the Promised Land peacefully and prosperously was conditional on them living as God would have them live. Blessings were for those who obeyed God. In calling the Temple **"a den of thieves,"** Jeremiah was confronting the hypocrisy of God's people in thinking they could be thoroughly pagan in every aspect of their lives and then pretend to come worthily into God's house (Matt. 21:13; Mark 11:17; Luke 19:46). Jeremiah 7:8 "Behold, ye trust in lying words that cannot profit." What they are discouraged from and acknowledged were introduced by contention and awareness. It was a specific thing they did and worthy of consideration and severe reflection. And it was astonishing that it was of no advantage to them but difficult.

"That cannot profit": Temple worship and service, legal sacrifices, and ceremonies could not take away sin and repay its guilt or justify men and render them acceptable to God. These, without faith in the blood and sacrifice of Christ, which was yet coming, were of no avail; and particularly could never be thought to be of any use and profit when such disgusting abominations were treated by them as are. They had believed lies. They had turned from God to these false gods. What could they possibly profit from an idol which is nothing?

Jeremiah 7:9 "Will ye steal, murder, commit adultery, swear falsely, burn incense unto Baal, and walk after other gods whom ye know not;"

At the same time, they offered sacrifices and trusted in them. They did those things that would not be pleasing to the Lord or useful to them. Or "ye do steal," the Septuagint, and all the versions; likewise, the Targum; as charging the people with them; these are sins against the second table of the law, as what follows are against the first.

Note: The "first table" is about how God's people should relate to God.

The second "table" is about how they should relate to their neighbors.

And burn incense unto Baal and walk after other gods whom ye know not": For they not only burnt incense to Baal, which was an act of idolatrous worship. But served other strange gods they had not known before. Whose names they had never heard of, and of whose help and assistance they had no experience; nor received any benefit from, as they had from the only true God. And therefore, it was great folly and ingratitude in them to forsake the Lord and walk after these.

Jeremiah 7:10 "And come and stand before me in this house, called by my name, and say, we are delivered to do all these abominations?"

In the temple, either as if they had done no such thing, like the whore, that wipes her mouth and says she hath done no wickedness (Prov. 30:20), noting their deep hypocrisy.

Or else that this would barely atone for all their abominations, as if they could make God amends for their sins by their duties, and their position of standing signifies their service (1 Kings 10:8; Prov. 22:29).

"We are delivered to do all these abominations": That is, because they had appeared before God with their sacrifices, either they thought themselves safe from all danger and freed from God's judgments (Mal. 3:15); or rather fortunate to return to all that wickedness again, at this moment noting their boldness (Isa. 1:12). They were not free to do these sins because they belonged to God. It is so much like many Christians today who believe they can live any way they want and not be guilty of sin because they have been baptized. Christianity is a daily walk in the footsteps Jesus left for us to walk in. We must continue in our salvation. When we receive the Lord, we are supposed to be brand new creatures in Christ.

We as people forget" **The Great White Throne Judgment." When the books are open, will your name still be listed in the books of life?** "Revelation 20: 11-15 Revelation 20:11 "And I saw a great white throne, and him that sat on it, from whose face the earth and the heaven fled away; and there was found no place for them."

"Great white throne": Nearly fifty times in Revelation, there is the mention of a throne. It is a judgment throne, elevated, pure, and holy **"Great White Throne – Judgment Seat."** God sits on it as judge (Rev. 4:2-3, 9; 5:1, 7, 13; 6:16; 7:10, 15) in the person of the Lord Jesus Christ (Rev. 21:5-6; John 5:22-29; Acts 17:31).

It is judgment hour now. Now John describes the terrifying scene set before him. He sees the Judge seated on His throne of Judgment and all the accused standing before Him. The verdicts handed down from this throne will be equitable, righteous, and just. The earth and the heaven fled away": John saw the diseased universe go out of existence. Peter described this second (2 Peter 3:10-13).

The universe is "uncreated," going into non-existence (Matt. 24:35; **"Destruction of the Earth by God."** We also remember (Ecclesiastes 12:14), which promises, "God shall bring every work into judgment, with every secret thing, whether good or evil." As well as (Romans 2:5-6), Paul speaks of the day of God's wrath "when his righteous judgment will be revealed. God will give to each person according to what he has done". It is a fearful thing even to imagine standing before God "from whose face the earth and the heaven fled away" and have nothing but your wicked works to show for the time on earth the Almighty had given you. On that day, the words of Paul the apostle will come true: "Now we know that whatever the law says, it says to those who are under the law so that every mouth may be silenced and the whole world held accountable to God" (Rom. 3:19). The ultimate word of course of action will be God's. This vision follows those of the Second Coming and those of the Millennium, immediately preceding the new heaven and new earth.

The use for the earth is over. The world, heaven, and everything in them are under God's control, and if He tells them to go, they will have to. It is an amazing, incredible statement explaining the creation of the universe. The earth was reshaped by the tribulation judgments, restored during the millennial kingdom; now God will create a new heaven and new world as it states (2 Peter 3).

2 Peter 3:13 "Nevertheless we, according to his promise, look for new heavens and a new earth, wherein dwelleth righteousness."

The "dead" are the unbelieving dead of all the ages, the "rest of the dead." They are "judged" from two sets of books (**"Book of Life –Another book- The Books of Damnation"**). The "books" contain the record of every unsaved person's life. Each unsaved person is judged following their "works" (Rom. 2:6, 16), which clearly shows that each one is a guilty sinner (Rom. 3:9-19), deserving of eternal death (Rom. 3:23; 6:23). **The "Book of Life"** contains the name of every person who has received eternal life through faith alone (John 20:31; 1 John 5:11-13).

These unsaved people are shown that they did not take advantage of the offer of eternal life through faith (Rom. 9:32; 10:3). **The Books of Damnation: Second Death - "Death and Hell" (Hades)** are the temporary holding places of unsaved men's bodies and souls, respectively (Luke 16:19-31).

Revelation 20:12 "And I saw the dead, small and great, stand before God; and the books were opened: and another book was opened, which is the book of life: and the book of damnation -the dead were judged out of those things which were written in the books, according to their works."

The "dead" are spiritually dead because they rejected Christ. They will stand in their resurrected state before Jesus to be judged by Him.

"Stand before God": In a judicial sense, as guilty, we are without excuses, condemned prisoners before the bar of divine justice. There are no living sinners left in the destroyed universe since all sinners were killed and believers glorified.

"Books": These books record every thought, word, and deed of sinful men, all recorded by divine omniscience (Dan. 7:9-10). They will provide the evidence for eternal condemnation.

These statements immediately call our attention back to the words of the Lord Jesus: "What you have said in the dark will be heard in the daylight, and what you have whispered in the ear in the inner rooms will be proclaimed from the roofs" (Luke 12:3). And "There is nothing hidden that will not be disclosed, and nothing concealed that will not be known or brought out into the open" (Luke 8:17).

Remember that the Christian dead have already won their victory. Those were judged by Jesus (**A Judgment Seat for Christians"**). Now is this final fearful scene, where these include all unbelievers who have ever lived. This is the resurrection of judgment, and they stand before Christ at the White Throne Judgment (**"Great White Throne Judgment Seat"**).

The capacity of the scene is horrifying. The great mass of these unbelievers before God's throne includes presidents and kings to paupers, prosperous, poor small, and excellent. There is no partiality with God as all will now face judgment.

"Books" is ("Book of Life – "Book of Damnation: Second Books"). Some books contain a person's every thought, word, and deed. Nothing will be hidden. Think about the fact that God knows the secrets of one's heart. Those who didn't accept Jesus will have to stand or fall on their deeds. Of course, they will all fall if they don't get

Him because all have sinned and come short of the glory of God. The Christian's sins have been done away with by the blood of Jesus.

God has kept perfect, complete, and accurate records of every person's life deeds, which will be measured against God's perfect and holy standard. Those who didn't accept Jesus will have to stand or fall on their works and deeds.

Of course, they will all fall if they don't get Him because scripture tells us that "all have sinned and come short of the glory of God."

"Book of Life": It contains the names of all the redeemed (Dan. 12:1; Dan 3:5). "Book of Damnation: Anyone not found written in the book of life cast into the lake of fire (Rev 20:15).

The Book of Life is the Lamb's Book of Life, where the names of all believers are written who have accepted, believed, and followed Christ. The Christian's sins have been done away with by the blood of Jesus. Those Christians all have their names written in the Lamb's book of life and will not taste the second death.

People are judged according to their deeds": Their <u>thoughts</u> (Luke 8:17; Rom. 2:16), **words** (Matt. 12:37), and **actions** (Matt. 16:27) will be likened to God's perfect, holy standard (Matt. 5:48; 1 Peter 1:15-16), and will be found wanting (Rom. 3:23). It also indicates that there are degrees of punishment in hell (Matt. 10:14-15; 11:22; Mark 12:38-40; Luke 12:47-48: Heb. 10:29).

Revelation 20:13 "And the sea gave up the dead which was in it, and death and hell delivered up the dead which were in them: and they were judged every man according to their works."

"Death and Hell "were cast into the lake of fire." Both terms describe the state of death. All unrighteous dead will appear at the Great White Throne Judgment; none will escape. All the places that have held the bodies of the unrighteous dead will yield up new bodies suited for hell, people who are lost wait in torment in an area of punishment until judgment day. The terrible thing is that they are aware that they will be thrown into the lake of fire on judgment day. These are all the unbelievers though all ages who have died. Christ will raise them for judgment called the second death. Before the sea was created and disappeared from existence, it gave up the dead in it. The sea may be mentioned as it is seemingly the most challenging place where dead bodies could be resurrected. But God will summon new bodies for all who perished in the sea throughout history.

Death represents all the places on land from which God will resurrect new bodies for the unrighteous, unrepentant dead.

The scene in this courtroom drama unfolds, and the lost will be assembled to appear before the judge. Since their deaths, their souls have been tormented in a place of punishment; now, the time has finally come for them to be judged and sentenced.

Revelation 20:14 "And death and hell were cast into the lake of fire. It is the second death. The "second death" is eternal punishment in the lake of fire, experienced only by the unsaved. Once this final judgment occurs, there is no further need for either death or hell (Isaiah 25:8; 1 Cor. 15:26-55). Eternal separation is made between those with life and death" (Dan. 12:2; John 5:29). It does not mean these places are hurled into the lake. It means the people of these places.

Revelation 20:15 "And whosoever was not found written in the book of life was cast into the lake of fire." The scriptures never refer to death as the end of life but instead as the unnatural separation of something from that to which it belongs. Therefore, a body without a spirit suffers physical death (Gen. 35:18). **The expression "second death" defines the separation of a man from God.** Human perception is expressed in the biblical description of the second death, suggesting that the beast and the False Prophet will remain alive for a thousand years after being cast into the lake of fire (19:20; 20:10). When a person is saved, he has passed from death to life and can be assured he will never come into condemnation (John 5:24; Gen. 2:17; Mark 9:43).

This absolute hell is described as the lake of fire. It exists but is presently not occupied until Satan, Beast, and the false prophet are thrown into the fire lake. They don't arrive there until the end of Tribulation.

Those who die in their sins in this world will die a second death in eternity. They will be sentenced to the lake of fire forever at the Great White Throne Judgment ("Judgment on Mankind is Coming").

Whether this fire is symbolic, the truth it signifies will be even more horrifying and painful. The bible also defines hell as a place of total darkness, which separates the unbelievers from the light and each other. What is recorded in these last two verses should drive us to continue spreading the gospel if there is breath in our bodies. I cannot bear to think of anyone I know going to this terrible place of torment. But it is their choice.

And that's it. In a ball of celestial flame, the rebellion is over. There will be no repeat of the plagues of the Tribulation nor of the judgments of the Great Tribulation. Humanity's rebellion will be wiped out of existence. It will be crystal clear to a watching universe that the death and resurrection of Jesus Christ are vital for making the unrighteous human heart into a vessel of God's holiness.

The Millennium will prove that even the best of conditions, a thousand years of peace, prosperity, safety, long life, health, and abundance, cannot change the wickedness of the unredeemed human heart. Only the Lord Jesus Christ can do that!

Excellent is the Word of God! It is probably impossible to reflect on these astonishing truths for extensive periods. Who can long consider the lake of fire, an eternal place of torment, possibly billions of unredeemed souls, a divine Person "from whose face the earth and the heaven fled away," or fearsome books of judgment that seal the fate of the unsaved?

And yet our Lord tells us of these remarkable events. To give us every chance to escape the terrible judgment that is to come. Remember, "no believer in Christ" will stand before God at the great white throne. That terrible spot is set aside only for those who have rejected Christ as Savior, decided to crown themselves king, and refused to accept Jesus Christ as their faithful Lord.

Do not make that terrible mistake! Instead, place your faith in the Lord Jesus and ask Him to forgive your sins; and repent then you will be ready "to stand before the Son of Man" at the judgment seat of Christ (Luke 21:36). One thing is sure: You will stand in one place or the other. Hell, or Heaven. Make sure it's the latter. And don't think that you can choose not to believe there is such a thing as heaven or hell as it makes no difference. Everyone will be judged and assigned to one place or the other. It is the same there; ignorance is no excuse for the law! Since the creation of the world, his invisible attributes are seen, being understood by the things that are made, even His eternal power and Godhead, so that they are without excuse (Romans 1:20, Romans 2:1). We are inexcusable; God takes no excuses, period. It is so easy to get your name written in the Lamb's book of life.

Romans 10:9-10 "That if thou shalt confess with thy mouth the Lord Jesus and believe in your heart that God hath raised him from the dead, thou shalt be saved."

"For with the heart man believeth unto righteousness, and with the mouth, confession is made unto salvation. You see, Jesus must be our Lord as well as our Savior. If you truly believe, you will repent and be baptized. If your name is not written in the book of life, do not delay, do it today. **Your Salvation" once you have**

The old sinful life should have been buried in the watery grave of baptism. We should be walking in the newness of life in Christ.

We no longer live, but Christ lives in us. It is the very same thing for these children of God. Their lives should reflect God within them. They should not live like the lost world.

Jeremiah 7:11 "Is this house, which called by my name, becomes a den of robbers in your eyes? Behold, even I have seen it, saith the Lord."

Only formal religious attendance at God's "house" is condemned by Jesus (Matt. 21:13; Mark 11:17; Luke 19:46). Because the house of God is to be a holy place. God never intended it to be a gathering place for thieves and robbers. Jesus spoke of it this way.

Matthew 21:13 "And said unto them, it is written, My house shall be called the house of prayer, but ye have made it a den of thieves."

God wants His people to be holy, as He is holy. He is our Tabernacle. He wants His people and His house to be holy and separated from the world. Christians should live holy lives because we bear the name of Christ.

Jeremiah 7:12 "But go you unto my place in Shiloh, where I set my name at first, and see what I did to it for the wickedness of my people Israel."

"Go unto Shiloh": God calls them to return to Shiloh, where the tabernacle dwelt along with the Ark of the Covenant. He permitted the Philistines to devastate that place.

"Shiloh" is an exciting word. It appears to be the place where the earliest sanctuary was located. It is in the same area as Shechem. It had been somewhat of a permanent structure to house the Ark of the Covenant. It had been destroyed.

Many of the people in and around Jerusalem did not believe God would allow the Babylonians to destroy the temple in Jerusalem. It reminds us that the first resting place had been destroyed, and Jerusalem would be no different.

The word "Shiloh" was not just a place but was also a name for the Messiah. Shiloh, the place was destroyed, and so will Jerusalem be destroyed by the Babylonians because of sin in their lives.

Jeremiah 7:13 "And now, because ye have done all these works, saith the LORD, and I spoke unto you, rising early and speaking, but ye heard not; and I called you, but ye answered not;."Rising early": This refers to the daily ministry of the prophets

"Rising early" becomes a common phrase in Jeremiah. The practice is in harmony with the consistent biblical teaching. Jesus, Himself rose before daybreak to pray (Mark 1:32-35). Many of God's choice servants had this practice (Gen. 28:16-22; Exodus 24:4-8; 34:4; 1 Sam. 1:19; 2 Chron. 29:20; Job 1:5).

The Psalms remind believers that the morning hour spent with God is vital for spiritual growth (Psalm 88:13). Each morning, God's child has a fresh opportunity to recall His mercy and protection (Psalms 59:16; 92:2) and find direction and guidance for the tasks of the day (Psalm 143:8). Jeremiah informs that the heavenly Father waited until it was early, awaiting a meeting with the citizens of Judah (7:25; 11:7-8; 25:3-4; 26:5; 29:19; 32:33; 35:14-15; 44:4-5). This phrase captures God's loving pursuit of His people, but they neither reacted nor met with Him (2 Chron. 36:15- 16).

Instead, as Zephaniah sadly reports, "They rose early and corrupted all their doings" (Zeph. 3:7) how great must be the heartbreak of God who earnestly longs to meet in communion and fellowship with His people, only to find that they do not keep their appointments with Him!

Everyone can do this in prayer!!! The earliest tabernacle from the wilderness period that had stood in "Shiloh" for so long had been abandoned.

Even the magnificent temple in Jerusalem, a solid and apparent sign of God's ongoing commitment to His people, would be as forsaken as Shiloh. God is never consulted by those who take Him for granted.

Jeremiah 7:14 "Therefore will I do unto this house, which is called by my name, wherein ye trust, and unto the place, I gave to you and your fathers, as I have done to Shiloh."

The temple for though His name called it, and His name was called upon, yet this could not secure it from desolation. For so the name of the Lord was set in the tabernacle at Shiloh, yet He forsook it because of the wickedness of the people.

"Wherein ye trust": They trusted in the sacrifices offered up there, and the services performed there; in the holiness of the place, and because it was the residence of the divine God; wherefore they thought this would be a protection and defense of them, and this was trusting in lying words (Jer. 7:4).

"And unto the place which I gave to you and your fathers": meaning either Jerusalem; the Syriac version renders it, "and to the city; or the whole land of Judea as in Jer. 7:7". "As I have done to Shiloh" :(Jer. 7:12).

God had warned them of the penalties of worshipping false gods. If they did not repent, he had Jeremiah tell them of their error and its liabilities. It appears the warning was not heeded. They had trusted in the temple being in Jerusalem forever. God had given them the Promised Land and dwelt with them in His temple in the Most Holy Place.

Jeremiah 7:15 "And I will cast you out of my sight, as I have cast out all your brethren, the whole seed of Ephraim." No observances, professions, or supposed revelations will profit if men do not amend their ways and doings. None should hope in free salvation, who allow themselves to practice known sin or live in the neglect of known duty.

They thought that the temple they desecrated would be their protection. But all who continue in sin because grace has thrived, or that grace may abound, make Christ the minister of sin; and the cross of Christ, rightly understood, forms the most helpful treatment to such poisonous attitudes.

The Son of God gave Himself for our transgressions to show the excellence of the Divine law and the evil of sin. Never let us think we may do wickedness without suffering for it.

Jeremiah 7:16 "Therefore pray not thou for these people, neither lift cry nor prayer for them, neither make intercession to me: for I will not hear thee."

"Pray not": God told His spokesman not to pray for the people. He did not find Judah leaning to repent. Instead, He saw the effective use of self-deceiving sayings and scandalous idol worship from a people unrelenting on not hearing.

God instructed Jeremiah not to "pray" for the people or "cry" over them. From youngest to oldest, they were intent on self-destruction, and God would let them have their way.

We see in this that God's judgment is already set. Jeremiah is not to pray for their deliverance because he would be praying against the will and judgment of God. We know that Abraham asked God to spare Sodom if He could find as many as ten righteous people. There were not ten honest, and God did not spare them. God told Abraham ahead of time that He would destroy them, but Abraham's prayers could not have stopped the judgment. No one can stop God's Judgment now. There are certain things God has planned. To intercede in prayer in opposition to God's plans will not work.

Jeremiah 7:17 "See thou not what they do in the cities of Judah and the streets of Jerusalem?"

We enter one of the darker regions of Jewish idolatry, such as Ezekiel saw in a vision. Foreign worship of the vilest kind was practiced, not only in secret but also in open places.

God brings Jeremiah's attention to the widespread sin in the cities. They must be punished for their sins. The punishment is to cause them to repent and turn to God.

Jeremiah 7:18 "The children gather wood, and the fathers kindle the fire, and the women knead the dough, make cakes to the queen of heaven, and pour out drink offerings unto other gods, that they may provoke me to anger."

"The queen of heaven": (Jer. 44:17-19, 25). The Jews worshiped Ishtar, an Assyrian and Babylonian goddess also called Ashtoreth, and Astarte, the wife of Baal or Molech. Because these deities symbolized procreative power, their worship involved prostitution (Judges 2:11-15).

We see from this that even the wives and children enter false worship with the fathers. It is an abomination before God. God is a jealous God; He will not tolerate the worship of other gods.

Deuteronomy 6:15, For the Lord thy God, a jealous God among us lest the anger of the Lord thy God is kindled against thee and destroy thee from off the face of the earth."

They are not only worshipping false gods but are doing it openly for all to see their unfaithfulness. God's fury has come up in His face against them.

Jeremiah 7:19 "Do they provoke me to anger? saith the LORD: do they not provoke themselves to the confusion of their faces?"

No: He cannot be provoked to anger as men are. Wrath does not fall upon Him as it does on men. There is no such anxiety in God as there is in men; His Spirit cannot be irritated and provoked in the manner that the spirits of men may be.

And though sin, especially idolatry, is disagreeable to Him, conflicting to His nature, and disgusting to His will, its damage is more to men themselves than to Him.

And though He sometimes does things like what men do when they are angry, there is no such anxiety in God as there is in men. Do they not provoke themselves to the confusion on their faces?": The most significant hurt that is done is to themselves. They are the sufferers in the end. They bring ruin and destruction upon themselves; and, therefore, have great reason to be angry with themselves since what they do brings their humiliation and embarrassment. The Targum says, "do they think that they provoke me? saith the Lord; is it not for evil to themselves, that they may be perplexed in their works?"

The answer is yes, and they do greatly provoke God. The worst thing is now they do not even know what they believe in. The "confusion of their faces" means they are bewildered in their worship. We had spoken earlier about their ritual of sacrificing to God still going on, but at the same time, they were worshipping false gods. They did not know what they believed.

Jeremiah 7:20 "Therefore thus saith the Lord God; Behold, mine anger, and my fury shall be poured out upon this place, upon man, and beast, and upon the trees of the field, and the fruit of the ground; and it shall burn, and shall not be quenched since these are their thoughts and this the fruit of their doings.

"Behold, mine anger, and my fury shall be poured out upon this place": Like fire, consume and destroy it, which was burned with fire; as a symbol of God's wrath, and an instance of His vengeance upon it, for their sins; which came down in great quantity, like a storm or hurricane.

"Upon man and upon beast": Upon beasts for man's sake, they are his property and use. Otherwise, they are innocent and do not deserve the wrath of God, nor are they aware of it.

"And upon the trees of the field, and upon the fruit of the ground": Which should be blighted by snapping winds or cut down and crushed upon by the Chaldean army.

"And it shall burn, and shall not be quenched": That is, the wrath of God shall burn like fire and shall not cease until it has executed the whole will of God in the punishment of His people.

These people were figuratively God's wives. There is nothing that makes a husband more furious than an unfaithful wife. They have been unfaithful to the Lord God. His anger will cause them to fall into this great battle with Babylon.

Deuteronomy 4:24 "For the LORD thy God a consuming fire, a jealous God.

Zechariah 8:2 "Thus saith the LORD of hosts; I was jealous for Zion with great jealousy, and I was jealous for her with great fury."

This destruction will be so great that the trees, fruit, and everything will be destroyed. As He regularly does, God invited His people to remember their past. The people had retained the practical rituals of "burnt offerings" and "sacrifices" while forsaking God's true commandment, "Obey My voice" (1 Sam. 15:22).

These verses do not diminish the importance of the Old Testament sacrifices. Still, they call attention to the requirement of the believer to live a life of total obedience and devotion to God. The Scriptures teach that religious rituals lacking spiritual commitment are worthless (1 Sam. 15:22-23; Psalm 40:6-8; Isa. 1:10-20; Micah 6:8).

Jeremiah 7:21 "Thus saith the Lord of hosts, the God of Israel; Put your burnt offerings unto your sacrifices and eat flesh."

The Lord of armies above and below, and the covenant God of the people of Israel, who were bound to serve Him. Not only by the laws of creation and the bounties of Divine intervention but were under agreement so to do by the unique blessings of His goodness bestowed upon them. Their idolatry, and other sins committed against Him, were the more heinous and worse.

"Put your burnt offerings unto your sacrifices, and eat flesh": Add one offering to another. Offer every kind of sacrifice, and, when you have done, eat the flesh of them yourselves.

For that is all the benefit that comes by them; they are not acceptable to me, as Jarchi observes; therefore, why should you lose them? Burnt offerings were solely eaten, and nothing was left of them to eat. But of other sacrifices there were, mainly the peace offerings, which the Jewish observers think are here intended by sacrifices; therefore, the people are bid to join them together, that they might have flesh to eat, which was all the benefit arising to them by legal sacrifices. The words seem to be mockingly spoken, showing the unacceptableness of legal sacrifices to God when sin was treated, and the lack of profitableness of them to men. God is telling them to go ahead and cook and eat the sacrifices they would have made to Him because they are unacceptable to Him. The Lord leaves no question about who He is here, stressing that He is the "God of Israel."

These offerings, sacrifices, Obey": Here is an essential emphasis on faithful obedience (Joshua 1:8; 1 Sam. 15:22; Prov. 15:18; 21:3; Isa. 1:11-17; Hosea 6:6; Matt. 9:13).

Jeremiah 7:22 "For I spoke not unto your fathers, nor commanded them in the day that I brought them out of the land of Egypt, concerning burnt offerings or sacrifices:"

"Nor commanded": Bible authors sometimes use the apparent inconsistency to make a practical meaning. What God commanded His people in the Exodus was not so much the offerings, as it was the faithful obedience that encouraged the offerings. (Deut. 5:3; Hosea 6:6; 1 John 3:18).

Jeremiah 7:23 "But this thing commanded I them, saying, obey my voice, and I will be your God, and ye shall be my people: and walk ye in all the ways that I have commanded you, that it may be well unto you."

It was the amount and substance of what was then commanded, even obedience to the moral law. It was the principal thing commanded and to which the promise was appropriated.

"Obey my voice": The word of the Lord, His commands, the precepts of the Ten Commandments. The obedience which was chosen to the sacrifices of the ceremonial law (1 Sam. 15:22), wherefore it follows:

"And I will be your God, and ye shall be my people": The meaning is that while they were obedient to Him, He would protect them from their enemies and continue them in their privileges and blessings, which He had granted to them as His unusual people. And walk ye in all the ways that I have commanded you": Not only in some but in all of them.

Not simply in the ritual of legal sacrifices but chiefly in the act of moral actions. Even in all the duties of religion, whatever is required in the law, respecting God or man.

"That it may be well unto you": They might continue in the land, which was given them for an inheritance, and enjoy all the blessings promised as a reward for their obedience.

We know that God promised blessings to His people if they obeyed Him and curses if they did not. It all began with the promises to Abraham. The decrees and laws God gave were for the benefit of man. The sacrifices were also for man to express thankfulness to God for the provisions God had made for him. Some of the sacrifices were to bring forgiveness for sins. All were for man's benefit. We will understand this better if we remember the great sacrifice that Jesus made for us. It was not for Jesus' benefit the sacrifice was made, but for men. If man had never fallen, there would have been no need for his sacrifice.

1 Samuel 15:22 "And Samuel said, Hath the Lord delight in burnt offerings and sacrifices, as in obeying the voice of the Lord? Behold, obey better than sacrifice, and hearken than the fat of rams."

To understand this more fully, we can study the book of Leviticus's six hundred and sixty laws. God will not be our God if we have other gods; he must be the only One, or He will not be our God.

Jeremiah 7:24 "But they hearkened not, nor inclined their ear, but walked in the counsels and the imagination of their evil heart, and went backward, not forward."

They were stubborn. "Went backward and not forward": The whole sacrificial system, even at its best, to say nothing of its idolatrous corruptions, was accordingly, from Jeremiah's point of view, a retrograde movement. The people's apostasy in the worship of the golden calf involved similar deflection, necessary and inevitable. However, it might be a process of education, from the first ideal government, based upon the covenant made with Abraham.

These are upon a pure and spiritual belief, the symbols and laws of which, though "hints of good things to come," were in themselves "weak and beggarly elements" (Heb. 10:1; Gal. 4:9). Man, by nature, is sinful. The instance of this that stands out to be the best is the children of Israel headed for the Promised Land. God miraculously brought them out of Egypt with the ten plagues He brought on Egypt. It alone should have convinced them that He was indeed God, and there were no others. He parted the Red Sea and took them over on dry land. He had Moses strike the Rock and water enough for the millions of people to spring forth. They still did not believe. They made the golden calf to worship. What does God have to do for a man before the man realizes who God is? It seems the man is so set on sinning that he ignores all the evidence and follows the desires of his flesh.

Jeremiah 7:25 "Since the day that your fathers came forth out of the land of Egypt, I have even sent unto you all my servants the prophets, daily rising early and sending.

That is, in all generations, ever since their first coming out of Egypt, they had been disobedient to the commands of God. And had walked after their own heart's lusts and gone backward, not forward. For this is not to relate to what follows: I have even sent unto you all my servants the prophets, daily rising early, and sending them": Which should be rendered, "although God has sent"; which is an annoyance of their sin, that they should continue in their disobedience. Though the Lord sent to them to encourage and warn them, not one, or two, of His servants, the prophets, but all of them, who daily rose early in the morning, which denotes their care and diligence to deliver God's message; and which, because they were sent of the Lord, and did His work as He directed them, it is attributed to Himself. And of these, there was a constant succession; from the time of their coming out of Egypt unto that day, which shows the goodness of God to that people, and their laziness, stiffness, and stubbornness. God heard their cry in Egypt and sent Moses to their rescue. God sent judges, prophets, and holy men, but they would not believe. They were so caught up in the desires of the flesh they would not listen to the warnings of God.

Jeremiah 7:26 "Yet they hearkened not unto me, nor inclined their ear, but hardened their neck: they did worse than their fathers."

He was speaking by the prophets. Inclined their ear": To what was said to them; would not listen to it, and much less obey what had commanded them. "But hardened their neck": And so, became stiff-necked, and would not submit to bear the yoke of the law.

"They did worse than their forefathers and fathers": Every generation grew more and more wicked and went on to be so until the measure of their iniquity was filled up. It seems the sins got worse with every generation. It was almost as if they were trying to outdo their fathers. The "hardening of their neck" meant they were too stubborn to learn.

Jeremiah 7:27 "Therefore thou shalt speak all these words unto them; but they will not hearken to thee: thou shalt also call unto them, but they will not answer thee."

Before mentioned in the chapter: appeals to duty, rebuking sins, promises, and threats. But they will not listen to thee: To reform from their evil ways and do the will of God. They will neither be tempted by promises nor intimidated by threats.

"Thou shalt also call unto them": With a loud voice, showing great intensity and earnestness. Being concerned for their good and knowing the danger they were in. But they will not answer thee": This the Lord knew, God all-knowing. And therefore, when it came to pass, it would be a confirmation to the prophet of his mission. And being told of it beforehand was prepared to meet with and expect such a reception from them. So that he would not be discouraged at it, and at the same time, it would confirm the role given to these people before. I feel so sorry for Jeremiah.

He brings the message from God to these people, and they will not listen or believe. How disappointing can this be? Noah had the same problem while he was building an Ark. He preached about the coming disaster but never had anyone believe him or change their ways. It is not the responsibility of the messenger to make them believe; it is enough that he brings God's message to the people. They have to believe.

CHAPTER 17

Judgment on Obscene Religion

Jeremiah 7:29-34

Jeremiah 7:29 "Cut off your hair, O Jerusalem, cast away, and take up a lamentation on high places; for the LORD hath rejected and forsaken the generation of his wrath."

"Cut off your hair": This is a sign explaining God's cutting the nation off and casting them into exile. Ezekiel used a similar illustration by cutting his hair (Ezek. 5:1-4). God never casts away the saved from spiritual salvation (John 6:37; 10:28-29).

"Cast it away": it is not to be reserved, as sometimes men and women do for some use; but to be cast away, and as good for nothing. And thus, it may agree with the church's lamentation (Lamentations 5:16), for it is not here encouraged as a token of repentance but as bad judgments.

They were to cut off their hair in mourning. It was a custom of the people when they took a Nazarite vow to grow their hair long and then cut it and cast it away. God has rejected and forsaken them. He wants no sacrifice to Him from them anymore.

Jeremiah 7:30 "For the children of Judah have done evil in my sight, saith the Lord: they have set their abominations in the house, which is called by my name, to pollute it."

Meaning not a single action only, but a series, a course of evil acts. And those openly, in a bold manner, not only before men, but in the sight of God, and contempt of Him, like the men of Sodom (Gen. 13:13).

"They have set their abominations in the house, which is called by my name, to pollute it": That is, they have set their idols in the temple. Even king Manasseh set up a graven image of the wood (2 Kings 21:7), which looked as if it was done to defile it.

It appears Manasseh had built altars for all the hosts of heaven. It is an abomination, a revolting sin in God's sight because the very first commandment is, **"Thou shalt have no other gods before me."**

The complete scriptural picture concerning this Canaanite abomination makes it clear that "Tophet" was a sacred enclosure in the "valley of the son of Hinnom," where the heinous child sacrifice burnt alive in the fire to a false god, Molech, was carried out (19:5-6; 32:35; 2 Kings 23:10; and 2 Kings 16:3-4 and 2 Chron. 28:3). Archaeological confirmation concerning the nature of the sacrifices carried out in Tophet comes from the excavations at the Phoenician colony of Carthage.

Jeremiah 7:31 "And they have built the high places of Tophet, which in the valley of the son of Hinnom, to burn their sons and their daughters in the fire, which I commanded not, neither came it into my heart."

"Burn their sons and their daughters in the fire": Though God forbade this evil (Lev. 18:21; 20:2-5; Deut. 12:31), Israelites still offered babies as sacrifices at the high places of idol worship (Tophet) in the valley of the son of Hinnom south end of Jerusalem. They offered them to the fire god Molech, believing that this god would reward them (19:6).

It is the worship of Molech which was strictly forbidden. They practiced the human sacrifice of their children to this false god.

Jeremiah 7:32 "Therefore, behold, the days come, saith the LORD, that it shall no more be called Tophet, nor the valley of the son of Hinnom, but the valley of slaughter: for they shall bury in Tophet, till there be no place."

"Valley of slaughter": God renamed the place because great slaughter would be forthcoming in the Babylonian invasion. We realize from this that this was common, and many children were killed. It would be correct to name it the valley of slaughter.

Jeremiah 7:33 "And the carcasses of this people shall be meat for the fowls of the heaven and the beasts of the earth, and none shall fray away."

Those which remain unburied, for which there will be found no place to bury them in. All areas, particularly Tophet, being so full of dead bodies; not to have a burial, which is here threatened, was accounted a great judgment.

"And none shall fray them away": or frighten them away. That is, drive away from the fowls and the beasts from the carcasses. The sense is either that there should be such a vast reduction of men that there would be no one left to do this, so the fowls and beasts might prey upon the carcasses without any disturbance. Or else, those left would be lacking humanity, as not to do this for the dead. In Deuteronomy 28:25, you can read of this very thing.

Jeremiah 7:34 "Then will I cause to cease from the cities of Judah, and the streets of Jerusalem, the voice of mirth, and the voice of gladness, the voice of the bridegroom, and the voice of the bride: for the land shall be desolate."

I was indicating that the destruction should not only be in and about Jerusalem but should reach all over the land of Judea. Since in all cities, towns, and villages, would cease: "The voice of mirth, and the voice of gladness": Upon any account whatever; and instead of that, mourning, weeping, and lamentation.

"The voice of the bridegroom, and the voice of the bride": No marrying, and giving in marriage, and so no expressions of joy on such occasions. And consequently, no likelihood at present of re-fill with the city of Jerusalem and the other cities of Judah.

"For the land shall be desolate": Without people to dwell in it and till it. The Septuagint, Syriac, and Arabic versions read, "The whole land."

The only thing we need to be reminded of here is that this punishment comes from God. Babylon may be the instrument that God uses to carry this out, but the judgment is from God. It is the curse God brings on His children who do not obey Him and who go after strange gods. It is speaking of annihilation. There would be no happiness at all, only desolation.

CHAPTER 18

The Lord Will Not Relent

Jeremiah 15:1-9

Jeremiah 15:1 "Then said the LORD unto me, Though Moses and Samuel stood before me, my mind not toward this people: cast out of my sight and let them go forth."In answer to his objections and appeals (Jer. 14:19).

"Though Moses and Samuel stood before me": To pray before me, as the Targum; to intercession for the people. Standing is a prayer movement. The Jews say there is no standing, but prayer or that is meant when mentioned; (Matt. 6:5). Moses and Samuel were named because they were eminent for worship and had success in it for the people of Israel. Of Moses (Exodus 32:11), Samuel (1 Sam. 7:9), and both (Psalm 99:6). But the words are only a belief and not a fact. The meaning is that supposing that Moses and Samuel were alive and made intercession for the people, their prayers would not be regarded.

"Yet my mind could not be towards this people": God could have no good will to them, no delight in them, and could not be reconciled to them or agree to it. The favors they asked for should have been granted, or they should be continued in their land. And therefore, it was in vain for the prophet to ask on their account. But, on the other hand, it is ordered as follows.

"Cast them out of my sight": Or presence; as persons despicable and horrific, not to be sustained. I cannot look upon them or have anything to say to them admiringly. "And let them go forth": From my presence, from the temple, the city, and out of their land. That is, declare that so it shall be.

Moses and Samuel were mighty men of God. God tells Jeremiah that even if they prayed for these people, He would say no. God has made His decision about the outcome of these people, and all the prayers in the world will not change God's plans. It is lovely to have someone to intercede on your behalf, but some things are set, and God will not alter them for anyone.

God is finished with them for the present. They have angered God beyond the point of His changing His mind. In the last chapter, he had told Jeremiah not to pray for these people anymore. Jeremiah is treading on the dangerous ground himself, disobeying God's command to him.

Jeremiah 15:2 "And it shall come to pass, if they say unto thee, whither shall we go forth? then thou shalt tell them, thus saith the LORD, Such as for death, to death; and such as for the sword, to the sword; and such as for the famine, to the famine; and such as for the captivity, to the captivity."

Suppose they ask thee what thou meanest by going forth. A term of motion suggests a period to which the action should be. Saith God, "in general, it is to ruin and destruction, but they shall not all be destroyed the same way." Some shall be destroyed by the pestilence, for that is here to be understood by death. The famine shall destroy others, others by the sword of enemies, others shall go into captivity. But one way or other, the land shall be relinquished of the most of you.

God is explaining to Jeremiah that the punishment for each of them is already set. Some of them will die, the sword will kill some, some will starve to death in the famine, and the rest will go into captivity. It is set, and there is no way to change it.

Jeremiah 15:3 "And I will appoint over them four kinds, saith the LORD: the sword to slay, and the dogs to tear, and the fowls of the heaven, and the beasts of the earth, to devour and destroy."

Or four families, and these very devouring ones. That is, four sorts of punishment; and so, the Targum, "four evil punishments," are mentioned. These are represented as under God and at his beck and call. Servants of his that go and come at his pleasure and do his will. And as being over men and having power and authority to kill and destroy by a divine commission. "*The sword to slay*": The first and chief of the four families or punishments, which had a commission from the Lord to scabbard itself in his people, the Jews. Even the enemy's sword, the Chaldeans, was drawn against them by divine order and appointment.

"And the dogs to tear": The carcasses of those slain with the sword. Or "to draw"; as the word signifies. It is the usual way for dogs to draw and drag the flesh they are feeding on. It is another of the four families and a very greedy one.

"And the fowls of the heaven, and the beasts of the earth, to devour and destroy": Or "to eat, and to corrupt," the bodies of those slain by the sword. The meaning is that such should not have burial but should be the food of fowls and wild beasts. These are the other two destroying families, which have their commission from the Lord for such service.

The sword will slay them, but they will not be buried. The dogs will get their bodies and drag them down the street. Vultures will eat the flesh off their bones. The beasts of the earth will get what the vultures do not.

Jeremiah 15:4 "And I will cause them to be removed into all kingdoms of the earth, because of Manasseh the son of Hezekiah king of Judah, for which he did in Jerusalem."

"Manasseh" was the grandfather of Josiah and one of Judah's worst kings. He worshiped idols over his fifty-five-year reign, filled Jerusalem with violence, and even sacrificed his son to the pagan gods (2 Kings 21). Judah's return to his evil ways following Josiah's godly reign made judgment unavoidable (2 Kings 24:3-4). We remember Manasseh as an evil king who caused the worship of many false gods. He even put-up statues of them. This same type of thing is found in the following Scriptures. "The Lord shall make the rain of thy land powder and dust: from heaven shall it come down upon thee until thou be destroyed." "The Lord shall cause thee to be smitten before thine enemies: thou shalt go out one way against them and flee seven ways before them: and shalt be removed into all the kingdoms of the earth." "And thy carcass shall be meat unto all fowls of the air and the beasts of the earth, and no man shall fray away (Deuteronomy 28:24-26).

Notice this is not Satan; this is judgment from God for worshipping false gods. For who shall pity thee, O Jerusalem? Or who shall bemoan thee? or who shall go aside to ask how thou does (Jeremiah 15:5)?

The inhabitants of it; their sins are so many, and so terrible, and so serious, and so deserving of punishment that none could pity their case, have a heart of compassion towards them, or even spare reproaching them. Or who shall mourn thee?" Sympathize and condole with thee, or speak a comfortable word to thee, or seek to relieve thy grief and sorrow. Who shall go aside to ask how thou does?" or "of thy peace?" Shall not think it worth their while to go a step out of their way, turn into a house, inquire of thy welfare, or salute thee. When God turns against them, no one is left to care what happens to them.

Jeremiah 15:6 "Thou hast forsaken me, saith the LORD, thou art gone backward: therefore, will I stretch out my hand against thee, and destroy thee; I am weary with repenting."

"I am weary with relenting": God often withholds the judgment He threatens (Exodus 32:14; 1 Chron. 21:15), saving men so that His patience might lead them to repentance (Rom. 2:4-5; 3:25).

From a human point of view, God's relenting of the threatened calamity against Judah may seem to be a change of mind. However, this "hand" will "stretch out' in judgment against them.

God had heard their cry for help so many times, and every time they repented, He had taken them back and blessed them instead of punishing them. This time will be different. They have gone too far. God will allow the punishment to happen.

Jeremiah 15:7 "And I will fan them with a fan in the gates of the land; I will bereave [them] of children, I will destroy my people, they return not from their ways."

Either of their land, the land of Judea. And so, the Septuagint version, "in the gates of my people,"; refers to the custom of sifting corn in open places. And by blowing means the distribution of the Jews, and they're being carried captive out of their land into other countries. Or the enemy's land, into their cities, as the Targum paraphrases it. Gates are being put for them frequently. Whither they should be scattered by the fan of the Lord; for what was done by the enemy, as an instrument, is credited to him. I will make an orphan them of children": Which shall die of famine, or pestilence, or by the sword, or in captivity. I will destroy my people, which must be when children are cut off. Families, towns, cities, and kingdoms are continued and kept up. And this he was determined to do, though they were his people. Since they return not from their ways": Their evil practices, which they had gone into, forsaking the ways of God, and his worship. Yet they return not from their ways": Though provoked with the fan of affliction, the mourning of their children, and threatened with destruction. It expresses their stubborn persistence in their evil ways and the reason for God's dealing with them as above.

Bereave in the Scripture above means miscarry or abortion. It just means that a woman with a child will miscarry that child because of the terrible hardships of war. When you fan a fire, you make it hotter. God causes this to become worse because of their sin. Their widows are increased to me above the sand of the seas: I have brought upon them against the mother of the young men a spoiler at noonday: I have caused to fall upon it suddenly, and terrors upon the city (Jeremiah 15:8). Translated, "I have brought upon them, even upon the young man's mother, a spoiler." The word rendered "young man" means a picked warrior. The mother has borne a brave champion, but neither his bravery nor the numerous offspring of the other can avail to save those who gave them birth. Therefore, the number of widows are significantly increased. Against the mother of the young men": Rather, upon young man., The widow has lost her husband, the mother her son so that no human power can repel the vicious adversary. The word rendered "young man" is used for "young warriors," (Jer. 18:21; 49:26; 51:3).

Others following Rashi take "mother" in the sense of "city." In which case, "young man" must relate to the deponent provided. A spoiler;" but though the word in (2 Sam. 20:19), it is there connected with "city," so that no doubt can exist. Hero the prophet would certainly not have used the word in so unusual a sense without giving some guide to his meaning. I have caused him": Rather, I have suddenly caused pangs and terrors to fall upon her. And horrors upon the city": Or "city and fears"; the city was immediately filled with terrors at the appearance of Nebuchadnezzar and his army. "An army and frights" (1 Sam. 28:16). At the head of his army, the Babylonian monarch spread terrors where he came. Some render the word, from (Dan. 4:13), "a watcher and dreads": meaning the Chaldean army, called watchers (Jer. 4:16). The Targum is, "I will bring an army upon them suddenly, and destroy their cities;" it should be executed as "separation of mind and fears." It is just speaking of the vast numbers of young men who die in the war. The destruction from this war is sudden and leaves tiny behind.

She that hath borne seven languished: she hath given up the ghost; her sun is gone down during day: she hath been ashamed and baffled: and the residue of them will I deliver to the sword before their enemies, saith the Lord (Jeremiah 15:9). In the picture of the earlier verse, the glory of the mother was found in the courage of her son, here in the number of her children. "Seven," as the perfect number, represented (1 Sam. 2:5; Ruth 4:15) the normal wholeness of the family. She hath given up the ghost": "blew out her soul." Her breath departs; no life can be kept in her. She faints away at the tragedies coming on her. Her son is gone down while it was the day": The blackness of suffering, and the evening of grief and disaster came upon her sooner than expected. At the same time, peace and prosperity were promised and hoped to be enjoyed for a long time (Amos 8:9).

She hath been embarrassed and baffled": Of her vain hope, trust, and confidence. "And the residue of them will I deliver to the sword before their enemies, saith the Lord": That is; such who died not of the famine and pestilence, but at the breaking up of the city struggled to make their escape. These fell into the hands of the enemy and perished by the sword, as the Lord here predicts. For whatsoever he says undoubtedly comes to pass. "*Languished*" means droop or be sick. It appears this sickness is to the death. It seems she died while she was still in her childbearing years. These verses contain Jeremiah's lamentations over his lot in life and his great loneliness. To these very human sorrows, the Lord has comforting replies: Jeremiah will be pardoned, and God's prophet will be fortified against danger under challenging times. Jeremiah once again mourned the suffering of his situation and the unfair persecution he suffered for his faithfulness to God's calling. The Lord does not promise that ministry is an easy life, but He does assure His servants that He will give them the strength to endure.

CHAPTER 19

The Branch of Righteousness

Jeremiah 23:1-8

Jeremiah 23:1 "Woe be unto the pastors that destroy and scatter the sheep of my pasture! saith the Lord."

The shepherd is a common metaphor for Israel's civil and spiritual leaders (Psalm 78:70-72; Ezek. 34). But these leaders have destroyed their flocks rather than protecting them and meeting their needs. Pastors are the same as a shepherd. Whether then or now, the false shepherd has no regard for the sheep. He is interested only in his welfare. The Scripture is speaking to the leaders of the people then and the leaders in our churches now. These false shepherds do; they scatter and destroy the sheep.

Jeremiah 23:2 "Therefore thus saith the Lord God of Israel against the pastors that feed my people; Ye have scattered my flock, driven them away, and have not visited them: behold, I will visit upon you the evil of your doings, saith the Lord."

"O ye shepherds" or "governors," The civil rulers and judges, kings, and princes of the land of Israel. Since religious rulers, priests, and prophets. Whose business it was to rule and guide, protect, and defend the people. But, instead of that, they were:

That destroy and scatter the sheep of my pasture, saith the Lord God": Set their bad examples and led them into idolatry and other sins, which were the cause of their ruin and carried captive and scattered in other countries. And their sin was the more severe because these people were the Lord's pasture sheep. He had an interest in and had committed them to the care and charge of these pastors or councils to be taken care of.

The Word of God is food. It is imperative to bring the Word of God in complete truth. Most people are influenced by the message the shepherd brings. If the statement is true, it brings the Lord life, health, and joy. If the message is not the truth, it brings death to the body and the soul. The statement "Lord God of Israel" lets us know that the crime against the evil shepherd is a false religion. Israel did not and did not have many gods. The Lord God is their only God. It is true of the Jewish nation who is physical Israel, and it is true of all believers in Christ. The leaders had scattered the people to the foreign lands with their false worship. **"I will gather"**: God pledged to restore exiled Israelites to their ancient soil. The land in view was accurately Palestine, compared with all the other countries, thus guaranteeing that the regathering would be as exact as the scattering. The restoration of Judah from Babylon is referred to in language, which in its fullness can only refer to the final restoration of God's people out of all the countries; "Nor will any be missing" indicates that no one will be missing or detached. These are prophecies not yet fulfilled (Isa. 60:21; Ezek. 34:11-16).

Jeremiah 23:3 "And I will gather the remnant of my flock out of all countries whither I have driven them and bring them again to their folds, and they shall be fruitful and increase."

That this prophecy looks beyond the returning exiles of Judah to the religious scene is clear from the worldwide scope of the situation. The prophets repeatedly predicted that God would regather His people in the distant future, that they would turn to Him and enter His millennial kingdom (Isa. 10:20-23; Ezek.36; 37:15-28; Joel 2:32; Micah 2:12-13; 4:1-8; 5:7-8; 7:18-20; Zech. 8:6-8).

God has always had a remnant of His people. It has more than one fulfillment. We know that the very thing this is speaking of happened at the end of the Babylonian captivity. The sheep came back to Israel. It also is in the process of coming about today in Israel.

In 1948, Israel became a nation, and ever since, Israelis from all over the world have been coming to the homeland. There seems to be a truth also to the fruitfulness of the Hebrews. They think children are a blessing from God. They also feel God has not looked kindly upon them when they do not have children. The Promised Land Israel is growing in population every day. Their people returned to Israel after many years of suffering and exile.

Jeremiah 23:4 "And I will set up shepherds over them which shall feed them: and they shall fear no more, nor be dismayed, neither shall they be lacking, saith the Lord."

The word "shepherds" is the same as that translated "pastors. Compared to Judah's wicked pastors, God will give His people a good One. The whole passage is taken from the descriptions of shepherding. As a Good Shepherd, God Himself will gather the scattered sheep of Israel and give them new shepherds who will serve under the Chief Shepherd of the flock (Isa. 10:20-22; Ezek. 34:22-24).

"Shepherds shall feed them" (Ezek. 34:23-31). Zerubbabel, Ezra, Nehemiah, and others were minor satisfactions associated with the absolute shepherding of the Messiah Jesus. The theme of the shepherd is a familiar one in the Scriptures. God assumed it as He led Israel (Psalm 80:1) while seeing to their needs (Psalm 23:1-2) and protecting and guiding them following His good purposes for them (Isa. 40:9-20 with Ezek. 34:12; Zech. 9:15-16). Israel's leaders were charged with caring for God's people as a shepherd would watch over his flock (Num. 27:17), but they often proved to be false shepherds (Ezek. 34:2; Zech. 10:2; 11:4). Accordingly, God announced through His prophets that He would send His true Shepherd, who would save and care for His flock (Ezek. 34:22-24). Christ affirmed that He was that Good Shepherd who, as a smitten Shepherd (Zech. 13:7), would lay down His life for the sheep (John 10:11).

According to Heb. 13:20-21 that Christ is also that Great Shepherd who sees the maturing and well-being of His believing flock (1 Peter 2:25). Peter confirms that Christ is the Chief Shepherd who has entrusted His work to other "under-shepherds" until He shall come again for His flock (1 Peter 5:4) so that it is no accident that one of the terms for the pastor in the New Testament means "shepherd" and that Paul could instruct the Ephesian elders in "shepherding" (Acts 20:17-38).

God had miraculously provided for the Israelites over and over. The forty years they wandered on their way to the Promised Land. God fed them with manna from heaven. God will choose men of good character to lead His sheep. The great Shepherd Jesus Christ is the authentic Shepherd. Others who watch over smaller flocks are under-shepherds to Him.

Jeremiah 23:5 "Behold, the days come, saith the LORD, that I will raise unto David a righteous Branch, and a King shall reign and prosper and execute judgment and justice in the earth."

"*Branch*": The Messiah is pictured as a branch is a shoot out of David's family tree (Isa. 4:2; 11:1-5; Zech. 3:8; 6:12-13), who will rule over God's people the future, where the same promise is repeated.

The phrase "the days come" refers to the messianic era when the "righteous Branch" (Zech. 3:8; 6:12 with Isa. 11:1) of the Lord (Isa. 4:2) will "grow up unto David."

The "*righteous Branch*" refers to the future Messiah who would be the rightful heir that would emerge from the Davidic line like a branch sprouting from a tree stump (Zech. 3:8; 6:12). Unlike wicked King Zedekiah, whose name means "*The Lord our Righteousness*," Jesus as Messiah will truly live up to His name and rule over His people in righteousness (Isa. 11:4-5).

It is a prophecy about the coming Messiah. Jesus Christ was their Messiah. He is the righteous Branch. He was the Lion of the tribe of Judah. He was of the house of David. His Father was God. When it speaks of His reign, it speaks of Him coming back to the earth as King of kings and Lord of lords. Jesus Christ is the righteous Judge.

Jeremiah 23:6 "In his days Judah shall be saved, and Israel shall dwell safely: and this his name whereby he shall be called, **THE LORD OUR RIGHTEOUSNESS.**"

- ❖ Messiah's shepherding is linked with that of the false shepherds.
- ❖ Judah and Israel will be reunited (Ezek. 37:15-23).
- ❖ The Messiah's title, "The Lord our Righteousness," will also be given to Jerusalem
- ❖ Because the Righteous One will be there (Ezek. 48:35; Joel 3:17, 21).
- ❖ In the Old Testament, God's name is recorded as being on the temple (1 Kings 8:43: 2 Chron. 6:33),
- ❖ The city of Jerusalem (Dan. 9:18),
- ❖ His people, both Israel (2 Chron. 7:14; Isa. 4:1; 63:19; Dan. 9:19),
- ❖ And among the Gentiles (Amos 9:12).
- ❖ Jeremiah also identifies himself by the title.

In the New Testament, that name becomes mainly associated with God's Son, Jesus Christ (Acts 5:41; 3 John 7; Rev. 2:13; 3:12; 22:4). There is the one-thousand-year reign of Jesus Christ as King and Lord. We know that there is more than one meaning for a prophetic Scripture many times. The Word of God could be speaking of Judah and Benjamin coming back to their homeland after their captivity. There has never been a time in the past when Judah was saved and Israel dwelled safely. There will come a time that Satan will be bound for a thousand years, and we who believe in Jesus will reign on this earth with Him.

Notice: This Special Name, THE LORD OUR RIGHTEOUSNESS. Jesus Christ is our righteousness. He will reign as Lord of lords and King of kings during this particular time. There will be perfect peace because the King of Peace will be here.

Jeremiah 23:7 Therefore, behold, the days come, saith the LORD, that they shall no longer say, The Lord lived, which brought up the children of Israel out of the land of Egypt.

"Are coming"; and will begin to take place in a bit of time, even upon the Jews' return from Babylon. And reached to the times of Christ, to which they have particular regard. Even the latter-day glory, the whole Gospel release when the Jews shall return to, and dwell in, their land (Jer. 23:8). That they shall no longer say, the Lord lived": The people of Israel in regard. Or the Lord's people shall no longer swear by the living God, described as follows. Declare no more the power of God, in the order next declared, and they had been used to do.

"Which brought up the children of Israel out of the land of Egypt": though a beautiful deliverance, and never to be forgotten, yet not to be named with the redemption and salvation wrought out by Christ the Lord our righteousness. That being deliverance from far greater and more powerful enemies and the far greater bondage of sin, Satan, and the law. Nor with the restoration of the Jews in the latter-day, which will be a most beautiful and fantastic event (Rom. 11:15).

Jeremiah 23:8 "But, The LORD lived, which brought up and led the seed of the house of Israel out of the north country, and from all countries whither I had driven them, and they shall dwell in their land."

Or they shall swear by the living God. Or declare the power of the Lord in their redemption by the Messiah.

Which brought up and which led the seed of the house of Israel out of the north country, and from all countries whither I had driven them": Which respects not only the deliverance of the Jews from Babylon, which lay north of Judea; but the transformation of many of the ten tribes. Through the preaching of the Gospel in the several countries where they were, to which the apostles of Christ were sent with it. The gathering of them together on the final day, when they shall turn to the Lord and return to their land as follows.

"And they shall dwell in their land, " which has never been fulfilled yet of the seed of the house of Israel or the ten tribes; but will be when all Israel shall be saved. This passage is about the days of the Messiah (Jer. 16:14-15).

God is not the God of yesterday; He is the great I AM. He is God of the present. He is alive. He eternally exists. Again, we see two meanings here. God did bring them out of Babylon back to Jerusalem. He is also getting them from the lands worldwide right now. They shall dwell in their lands.

CHAPTER 20

The Army of Hell

Ephesians 6:12

Ephesians 6:12 "For we wrestle not against flesh and blood, but against principalities, against powers, against the rulers of the darkness of this world, against spiritual wickedness in high places."

- ❖ *Principalities:*
- ❖ *Powers:*
- ❖ *Rulers of darkness:*
- ❖ *Spiritual forces of wickedness:*

"Wrestle": Wrestle or struggle is used for hand-to-hand combat with your sword; struggling or wrestling includes trickery and deception, like Satan and his hosts when they attack. Coping with deceptive temptation requires truth and righteousness.

Principalities: They are the top-ranking demonic beings; they are the chief of the hierarchy. These chief demons communicate with the archangels among the holy angels in war. These princes hold sway over the soul of people. A principality is what assigns demonic spirits to operate in the disobedient; these princes rule over continents and nations. These demons are subject to Christ and subject to spirit-filled believers.

Powers: are another rank of evil offices in armor suits of darkness; they delegate authority like a drill sergeant. These demons operate invisibly in government centers such as the national government for the sake of power. This power cannot separate us from the love of God. These powers will be shaken at the end of the age. All these powers, and principalities, are subject to Christ (1 Pet. 3: 22). And world forces of this darkness perhaps refer to demons who have penetrated countless world political systems, attempting to emulate them after Satan's realm of darkness (Dan. 10:13; Col. 1:13).

The spiritual forces of wickedness are possibly those demons involved in the most wretched and vile immoralities, such as highly perverse sexual activities, the occult, Satan worship, and the like.

The purpose here is not to describe the details of the demonic hierarchy but to give us some idea of its difficulty and power. We are pitted against an extraordinarily evil and efficient enemy. But our need is not to openly recognize every feature of our adversary but to turn to God, our influential and trustworthy source of protection and victory.

Several activities in the Bible may involve demons. Sometimes they cause physical disease or mental suffering. However, not all mental disorders are demonic in origin. Demons also tempt people into immoral practices. They originate and spread false doctrines taught by demons (Mark 1:23). Although demons are committed to doing evil, God will use them to accomplish His plan during the end of the age (Rev. 16:14).

Demons are also objects of worship in various occult practices forbidden by God. These include:

- *divination* is an unlawful means of controlling the will of God
- *necromancy* efforts to communicate with and interrogate the dead,
- *magic*-using formulas and incantations,
- *sorcery*, perhaps the non-medical use of drugs,
- *witchcraft, and astrology* (Deut. 18:10-12).

In one's Christian life, dealing with demons is not finding the technique to send them away but being committed to the spiritual means of grace that purifies the soul. There is no unclean place that demons could occupy or by which they might gain an advantage. James gives the only formula for deliverance from the demons or the devil himself: *"Resist the devil, and he will flee from you" (James 4:7).*

When the Ephesian Christians who were "experimenting" in the occult repented, there was a great revival in that place. No Christian can ever justify his participation in demonic activities (Exodus 7:11; Hebrew 1:4).

- ❖ *"Wrestle,"* used of hand-to-hand combat with your sword, highlights the personal and individual nature of spiritual warfare against each local church and Christian. "Flesh and blood" refer to humanity. Instead, she opposed:
- ❖ "Principalities -rulers,
- ❖ "powers" -authorities,
- ❖ rulers of darkness-world rulers,
- ❖ "Spiritual wickedness -wicked spiritual beings,
- ❖ That is fallen angels, demons, and Lucifer himself.

We must do to fight against our enemy to learn who he is and what his tactics are. We do this with daily prayer. The enemy that you cannot see is the hidden enemy is the most dangerous; the one you see with your physical eye is threatening because you do not know when he is on the attack or just which way he is coming from.

It is a spiritual battle, spoken of here with the holy spirit and prayer; you can stay ahead of the enemy. The devil -Lucifer and his angels, these demonic or devil spirits, are the enemy. His tactics are to tempt the flesh of man because we are earthy. These are real battles.

The Father has delivered us from the realm of darkness and transferred us to the kingdom of His beloved Son (Col. 1:11-13). No Christian is any longer in Satan's domain, and every Christian has the means of God's own Holy Spirit within him to free himself from any demonic entanglement, no matter how severe. Satan and his demons are banished where sin is admitted and put away. We are to put on The Whole Armor of God and Pray to Him; this is our way of communicating with him, then we have perfect confidence in the knowledge that "greater is He who is in us than he who is in the world" (1 John 4:4). The very "gates of Hades shall not overpower" Christ's church (Matthew 16:18).

"Rulers of the darkness; To seize and take hold of governments for darkness and evil. There are diverse divisions and rankings of those demons and the evil, the supernatural territory they operate. Human beings who promote paganism, the occult, and several other ungodly and immoral movements and programs are. Still, the victims of Satan and his demons, trapped by sin, are unwittingly helping to fulfill his plans. These demonic leaders touch the created order and arrangement. The rulers want to take over government offices, legislatures, congress, judges, and courts. The demonic classifications are not explained, but rulers undoubtedly reflect a high order of demons linked with "authorities" (Col. 2:15).

"Spiritual wickedness": Refers to the most depraved abomination, including such things as extreme sexual perversions, occultism, and Satan worship. They are spiritual fakes; the word wicked is potential, from which we get fornication and pornography. These are the unclean spirits we deal with daily.

Some of these spirits are named for us:

- ❖ *Beelzebub: the lord of flies*
- ❖ *Abaddon or Apollyon: the destroyer*
- ❖ *Demon: torment the mind*
- ❖ *Legion: six thousand or more demons (an army)*

The lower-level spirits are called *"imps."* They are minimal; sometimes, they try to choke you in your sleep, and they can make themselves appear very large; these are the ones we deal with daily. Satan's army is well organized, and his legions utilize a procession of tactics and schemes. We must be prepared to face this interior enemy and expose his tactics. "*In high places* refers to the entire realm of spiritual beings.

There are Eight Parts to their War Armor:

The Devil of Strife: Where envy and strife exist, confusion and evil will be there. (James 3: 16).

- ❖ The Helmet of Pride
- ❖ Breastplate of Unrighteousness
- ❖ Sword of Bitterness
- ❖ Shield of Hate
- ❖ Hammer of Judgement
- ❖ Cloak of Deception
- ❖ Boots of Anger
- ❖ Speaking Forth Lies

The eight parts of armor illustrate the different divisions and rankings of those demons and the evil supernatural kingdoms, nations, continents, governments, legislature, congress, Judiciary, territory, province, world power, and confederation in which they operate. Satan's forces of darkness are highly systematized for the most destructive functions (Col 2:15; 1 Peter 3:22).

We are reminded daily that the Christian's struggle is against Satan himself and a host of his demonic hierarchy, subordinates, officers, imps, and armed soldiers, a massive procession of adversaries who, like the devil, are not flesh and blood. Our greatest enemy is not the world we see, corrupt and wicked, but the world we cannot see. It is the enemy you do not see. The hidden enemy. "Not against flesh and blood" (2 Cor. 10:3-5).

CHAPTER 21

The Army of God

Ephesians 6:11-20

The Whole Armor of God

Ephesians 6:11 "Put on the whole armor of God, that ye may be able to stand against the devil's wiles."

"Put on the whole armor of God": "Put on" communicates the idea of stability, indicating that armor should be the Christian's maintained lifelong attire. These are soldiers armed to stand their ground in the believer's spiritual defense and acknowledge its necessity if one is to hold his position while under attack. There are four kinds of soldiers in God's Army:

- ❖ *Soldier #1*: These spiritual soldiers are made up of those who know nothing about the armor of God. Not only are they constantly being beaten up by the enemy. They often beat up other Christians with criticism, gossip, and complaints.
- ❖ *Soldier #2*: These spiritual soldiers are those who know the armor of God, but they refuse to wear it. They prefer to fight on their own and with their weapons instead. It is foolishness; it always leads to defeat.
- ❖ *Soldier #3*: There spiritual soldiers are those who wear some, but not all, the armor. They may have some victory in half of their lives and be victorious half of the time, but they are always half exposed and vulnerable to the enemy's attack.
- ❖ *Soldier# 4*: These spiritual soldiers cover those Christians who wear the entire armor of God and know how to use it. The

soldiers have battles daily, just like everyone else. They have fewer battles of defeat, and they come through victoriously.

We as soldiers must take advantage of the strength of God's might; a believer must also put on the whole spiritual armor that He supplies (2 Cor. 10:3-5). "Put on" carries the idea of once and for all, or stability. The armor of God is not something to be put on and taken off sometimes but is something to be put on permanently.

It is to be the Christian's lifelong acquaintance. It provides believers with divine power from "Him who can keep you for stumbling and make you stand in the presence of His glory blameless with great joy (Jude 24). "Put on" denotes a sense of urgency, demanding immediate action. *"To stand" has military overtones.* To resist the enemy and hold a critical position in battle. *"The wiles of the devil"* or "the Devil's strategy": Satan carefully devises schemes and tactics against believers.

- ❖ *"Wiles"*: Wiles or schemes carry the idea of cleverness, crafty methods, cunning, and deception. Satan's schemes stretch out through the corrupt world system he rules and carries out by his demonic hosts. "Wiles" surrounding every sin, immoral practice, false theology, false religion, and worldly enticement.
- ❖ *"Schemes"* carries the idea of craftiness, cunning, and deception. The term of a wild animal that cunningly stalked and then suddenly pounced on its prey. Satan's evil schemes are built around sneakiness and deception.
- ❖ Christians are really in a war. We are soldiers in God's army. The greatest battle is between the flesh and the spirit. The prize they are after is the soul or the will of man.

Paul said in the scripture while he was chained to a soldier, it was not difficult for him to use the armor of a soldier ready for battle as an example of what we must wear as armor in God's army.

"The devil": Scripture says:

- ❖ *"The anointed cherub" (Ezek. 28:14),*
- ❖ *"The ruler of the demons" (Luke 11:15),*
- ❖ *"The god of this world" (2 Cor. 4:4),*
- ❖ *"The prince of the power of the air" (Eph. 2:2).*
- ❖ *Scripture shows him opposing God's work (Zech. 3:1),*
- ❖ *Perverting God's Word (Matt. 4:6).*
- ❖ *They are hindering God's servant (1 Thess. 2:18).*
- ❖ *Hindering the gospel (2 Cor. 4:4*
- ❖ *Snaring the righteous (1 Thess. 3:7).*
- ❖ *He is holding the world in his power (1 John 5:19).*

This fallen archangel and his fallen angels, who became demons, have been tempting and corrupting humanity since the Garden of Eden. They are evil, intimidating, cunning, powerful, and invisible foes against whom no human being in his power is a match. There are daily conflicts with the devil and his army in this life. There are daily spiritual wars between armor-suited demons and God-armored archangels. Life is a battleground. Preparation is necessary to fight any battle. Jesus fought the devil with the Word of God. Our strength is in Bible daily in prayer.

Evidence of Satan's great power and deception can be seen in the fact that, despite God's miraculous deliverance of Israel from Egypt, His immeasurable blessings, protection, and provision in the wilderness and Canaan, His chosen people repeatedly fell for Satan's seductions, worshiping the hideous and demonic idols of paganism. After all the prognostications of the Messiah given in the Old Testament and after Jesus' preaching, teaching, and miraculous healings, Satan provoked Israel to reject and crucify her own Messiah! In the last days, his final deception of Israel will be to convince the world's people that the antichrist is instead the Christ (Dan. 9:26-27).

The demonic categories:

- *Rulers,* no doubt, reflect a high order of demons with "authorities" and "chiefs' demons" (Col. 2:15).
- *Powers are another rank (1 Peter 3:22).*
- *World forces of this darkness* signify demons penetrating various world political systems, attempting to pattern them after Satan's realm of darkness (Dan. 10:13; Col. 1:13).
- *Spiritual forces of wickedness* maybe those demons involved in the most wretched and vile immoralities, as extremely perverse sexual activities, the occult, Satan worship, and the like.
- It explains the details of the demonic hierarchy but gives us some idea of its complexity and power. We are pitted against an incredibly evil and potent enemy. But our need is not to specifically recognize every aspect of our adversary but to turn to God, our influential and trustworthy source of protection and victory.

Several activities in the Bible may involve demons. Sometimes they cause physical disease or mental suffering. However, not all mental disorders are demonic. Demons also tempt people into immoral practices. They create and spread false doctrines taught by demons (Mark 1:23). Although demons are committed to doing evil, God will use them to accomplish His plan in the end (Rev. 16:14).

Demons are also objects of worship in various occult, voodoo, enchanters, charmers, observers of times, sorcerers, witches, and wizards' practices forbidden by God. These include:

- *Divination is an illegitimate means of determining the will of God.*
- *Necromancy efforts to communicate with and interrogate the dead*
- *Magic using formulas and incantations*
- *Sorcery nonmedical use of drugs*

❖ *Witchcraft and astrology (Deut. 18:10-12).*

In one's Christian life, dealing with demons is not finding the technique to send them away but being committed to the spiritual means of grace that purifies the soul. There is no unclean place that demons could occupy or by which they might gain benefit. James gives the only formula for deliverance from the demons or the devil himself: *"Resist the devil, and he will flee from you" (James 4:7).* When the Ephesian Christians who were "experimenting" in the occult repented, there was a great revival in that place. No Christian can ever justify his participation in demonic activities (Exodus 7:11; Hebrew 1:4).

We must do to fight against our enemy to learn who he is and what his tactics are. The enemy that you cannot see with your physical eye is the most dangerous; he is the hidden enemy. Because you do not know when he is on the attack or just which way he is coming from. Our Father has delivered us from the realm of darkness and transferred us to the kingdom of His beloved Son (Col. 1:11-13). No Christian is any longer in Satan's domain. Every Christian has the armor of God's own Holy Spirit within him to free himself from any demonic entanglement, no matter how severe. Satan and his demons are banished where sin is admitted and put away.

We are to put on God's armor and communicate to Him, utterly confident in the knowledge that "greater is He who is in us than he who is in the world" (1 John 4:4). The very "gates of Hades shall not overpower" Christ's church (Matthew 16:18).

Ephesians 6:13 "Wherefore take unto you the whole armor of God, that ye may be able to withstand in the evil day, and having done all, to stand."

Because we face such a challenging foe, we must avail ourselves of God's provision in case the enemy destroys our Christian witness and ministry. "We must take unto us the whole armor of God": Paul again emphasized the requirement of the Christian's assuming God's full spiritual armor by obedience in taking it up or putting it on.

It is possible to live the Christian life in tiredness, disinterest, and perfect satisfaction with the way things are and still spend eternity with the Lord. Because He has eternally secured the salvation of every believer (John 10:28-29), we cannot lose the supreme war because we belong to the Lord and the battle is His.

But we ignore obedience to Him at a considerable cost. We bring our heavenly Father, and ourselves sorrow instead of joy. We leave lost souls in darkness and damnation instead of bringing them to the light of salvation. And we see our work damaged up with fires like so much straw, as we lose the reward that faithful service would bring.

The first three pieces of armor:

- ❖ *Girdle*
- ❖ *Breastplate*
- ❖ *Shoes/Boots* were worn continually on the battlefield.
- ❖ *Shield*
- ❖ *Helmet*
- ❖ *Sword* was kept ready for use when actual fighting began.

"The evil day": "Having done all, to stand": Standing firm against the enemy without hesitating or falling is the goal.

"The evil day" the continuing demonic onslaughts and satanic assaults. "Having done all" includes covering oneself in God's armor and resisting Satan. Having done all these, be ready, for the Devil will attack again and again. Since the fall of man, every day has been evil, a condition that will persist until the Lord returns and establishes His righteous kingdom on earth. This evil day is many different days. The battle sometimes stops for a day or two, but it starts again when you least expect it. Our job is to be ready, stay ready daily, and then stand.

The soldier's job is to stand and remain standing regardless of what the enemy sends your way. Our strength in this battle must come from God and the Holy Spirit. Christ in us gives us the power to stand firm in the war.

But even the most willing and eager soldier of Christ is helpless without God's provision. We have His prerequisite in being His children, having His Word, keeping His indwelling Holy Spirit, and having every armor of our heavenly Father. God is our strength, but His strength is assumed only through obedience; His mighty armor must be put on and taken up.

Some believers have done everything well in the Lord's work, but they do not continue to stand firm in prayer and read his Word. The issue is not in what a believer has done, but when the battle is over, and the smoke clears, whether we are found standing true to the Savior.

The whole armor of God consists of six pieces.

1. "*Truth* "is a knowledge of the truth of God's Word. The ancient soldiers' "loins" "waist" was "girt about" with a leather belt which kept most of the pieces of his armor in place. The other pieces of the Christian's armor depend on and are held in place by his spiritual "belt" or his knowledge of the "truth" of Scripture.

2. "*The Breastplate of righteousness* is "the breastplate which is righteousness." It represents a holy character and moral conduct. Obedience to the "truth" known produces a godly life righteousness."

3. "*Preparation of the gospel of peace* "eagerness that comes from the gospel of peace." That is, as the soldier wore special shoes called caligae on his feet, enabling him to advance against his enemy, so the Christian must have on his feet acquire, as a sense of "eagerness" or "willingness" to advance against the Devil and take the fight to him. Such "eagerness" to contend with Satan "comes from the gospel of peace." The gospel gives peace to the believer, freeing him from anxiety though he advances against such a powerful opponent.

4. *"The shield of "faith"* taking God at His word by believing His promises. Such trust will protect one from doubts caused by Satan.

5. *"The helmet of salvation* since the person who reads are already Christians they are not here persuaded to be saved. (1 Thessalonians 5:8), explains this helmet as "the hope of salvation," that is, the assurance of salvation.

6. *"The sword of the Spirit,* which is the word of God. The "Word" does not discuss the whole Word of God, but rhema, which talks about certain sections or particular verses of Scripture.

Ephesians 6:14 "Stand therefore, having your loins girt about with truth, and having on the breastplate of righteousness;."

"*Stand therefore*": The apostle calls Christians to take a firm position in the spiritual battle against Satan and his minions (Eph. 6:11, 13).

Satan attacks believers through wrong teaching, confusion, and falsehood. Christians who are untaught in God's Word fall easy prey to false beliefs about the things of God, about salvation, sanctification, morality, heaven, hell, the second coming, and every other biblical truth. The believer confused about God's Word cannot be successful in God's work. He is "tossed here and there by waves and carried about by every wind of wrong teaching. (Eph. 4:14).

Whether confronting Satan's effort to distrust God, forsaking obedience, producing biblical confusion and falsehood, hindering service to God, bringing division, serving God in the flesh, living hypocritically, being worldly, or in any other way rejecting biblical obedience, this armor is our defense.

Such as, when a young child dies or is forever crippled, a husband or wife is taken away, a child turns away from the Lord, or we lose a soul, job, or health, Satan or his demons may attempt to generate thoughts in the mind that place the blame on God. This field of conflict also involves attacking the truthfulness and competence of Scripture.

"Girt with the truth": The soldier wore a tunic of loose-fitting cloth. Since ancient combat was primarily handed to hand, a loose tunic was a possible hindrance and danger. A belt was required to cinch up the loosely hanging material. Girding up was a matter of pulling in the loose ends as preparation for battle. The strap that stretches all the spiritual loose ends is "truth" or "truthfulness." The notion is a sincere commitment to fight and win without hypocrisy, self-discipline, and devotion to victory. Everything that hinders is tucked away; (2 Tim. 2:4; Heb. 12:1). We are to be firmly secure in the Truth of God. We are to hold fast to the Truth.

"The breastplate of righteousness": The breastplate was usually rigid, without sleeves, leather, or heavy material with animal horn or hoof pieces sewn on, covering the soldier's entire torso, protecting his heart and other vital organs. Because righteousness or holiness is such a distinct attribute of God Himself, it is not hard to understand why that is the Christians' chief protection against Satan and his schemes. The breastplate of righteousness that we use as spiritual armor against our adversary is the practical righteousness of a life that is lived in obedience to God's Word. The putting on of righteous behavior is in line with the "new self" (in 4:24-27), which, having been done, will "not give the devil an occasion." As believers faithfully live in obedience to and communion with Jesus Christ, His righteousness generates daily, daily righteousness that becomes their spiritual breastplate. On the other hand, lack of holiness leaves them weak to the great enemy of their souls (Isa. 59:17; 2 Cor. 7:1; 1 Thess. 5:8).

Being filled with God's Word but not obedient to His Spirit has caused the downfall of many believers. The right Word of God without the proper devotion is a major pitfall for many Christians. The person who trusts in his understanding instead of the Lord Himself (Proverbs 3:5) plays into Satan's hands. Within a few years, this very church at Ephesus became cold and systematic in the example of its accepted belief. Right religion without a deep devotion to Christ cannot prevent the death of a church. Putting on the breastplate of righteousness is to live in daily obedience to our heavenly Father, minute by minute. This part of God's armor is holy living for which God distributes the standard and the power but for which we must provide the willingness. God Himself puts on our assigned righteousness, but we must put on our everyday holiness. First, not being armored with the breastplate of righteousness will cost the Christian his joy. John's first epistle includes many warnings and commands to believers, and these are given, along with the other truths of the letter, "so that our joy may be made complete" (1 John 1:4).

In other words, a lack of obedience brings a lack of joy. The only joyful Christian is the obedient Christian. The saying is once saved, not always saved. Unholy living does not rob us of salvation, but it robs us of salvation's joy. The breastplate covers the heart. The righteousness that we have is the righteousness of Christ. We are clothed in His righteousness. His precious blood shed for humanity made us righteous and in right standing with God.

We have a brand-new heart washed in the blood of the Lamb. The nature of the Christian has the law of God engraved into the fleshly part of the heart. Our compassion has stayed upon God.

Ephesians 6:15 "And your feet shod with preparing the gospel of peace."

"Shod with … gospel of peace": Roman soldiers wore combat boots to grip the ground in combat. The gospel of peace concerns the good news that, through Christ, believers are at peace with God, and He is on their side (Rom. 5:6-10).

A Christian's spiritual footwear is uniformly essential in his warfare against the devil's schemes. Suppose he has carefully girded his loins with truth and put on the breastplate of righteousness but does not adequately shod his feet preparing the gospel of peace. In that case, he is predestined to stumble, fall, and suffer many defeats. Training has the general meaning of readiness. In this section, the gospel of peace refers to the good news that believers are at peace with God. The unsaved person is helpless, ungodly, sinful, and an enemy of God (Romans 5:6-10). On the other hand, the saved person is prepared to accept God through faith in His Son (Eph. 6:10-11). That confidence in divine support allows the believer to stand firm, knowing that God is his strength since he is at peace with God (Romans 8:31, 37-39).

Our feet are secure in the good news of the gospel. In Leviticus, we find that the right foot's big toe was covered in the blood so that our walk was pure before God. It means that our walk is steadfast, grounded, and secure in the good news of Jesus Christ.

The believer who stands in the Lord's power need does not fear any enemy, even Satan himself. When he comes to attack us, our feet are rooted firmly on the solid ground of the gospel of peace, through which God transformed from our enemy to our defender. We who were once His enemies are now His children, and our heavenly Father offers us His complete resources to "be strong in the Lord, and the strength of His might" (Eph. 6:10).

Ephesians 6:16 "Above all, taking the shield of faith, wherewith ye shall be able to quench all the fiery darts of the wicked."

"Above all" introduces the last three pieces of armor. The first was for long-range groundwork and protection and was never taken off on the battlefield. The shield, helmet, and sword, on the other hand, were kept in readiness for use when actual fighting began, so the verbs (Eph. 6:16-17), take on and take up.

"*The shield of faith*": The Greek word usually refers to the large shield protecting the entire body. The faith to which Paul refers is not the body of Christian teaching as the term is used, but essential trust in God, the belief in Christ that assumes salvation and continues to bring blessing and strength as it trusts Him for daily provision and help. The believer's constant trust in God's word and promise is necessary to protect him from desires to every sort of sin. All sin comes when the victim falls to Satan's lies and promises of pleasure, rejecting the better choice of obedience and blessing. The substance of Christianity believes that God exists and that He rewards those who seek Him (Heb. 11:6); putting total trust in His Son as the crucified, buried, risen, and risen Savior; obeying Scripture as His trustworthy and respected Word; and looking forward to the Lord's coming again.

"*Fiery darts*": Temptations are likened to the flaming arrows shot by the enemy and extinguished by the oil-treated leather shield (Psalm 18:30; Prov. 30:5-6; 1 John 5:4). The spiritual flaming missiles against which believers need protection would seem mostly to be temptations.

Satan continually overwhelms God's children with temptations to immorality, hatred, envy, anger, covetousness, perversion, homosexuality, pride, doubt, fear, despair, distrust, and every other sin. Therefore, the purpose of all of Satan's missiles is to cause believers to forsake their trust in God, to drive a wedge between the Savior and the saved. Without *faith*, it is impossible to please God. Our faith in God causes us to be able to ward off attacks from the devil and his crowd. If needed, we should have so much faith that we could move a mountain of problems. Let us look at Abraham, the father of faith, and see what God promised him.

Genesis 15:1 "After these things, the word of the LORD came unto Abram in a vision, saying, Fear not, Abram: I am thy shield, and thy exceeding great reward." Faith then is the shield.

Ephesians 6:17 "And take the helmet of salvation, and the sword of the Spirit, which is the word of God:"

"*The helmet of salvation*": The helmet protected the head, always a significant target in battle. Paul is speaking to those already saved and is therefore not talking here about getting salvation. Instead, Satan seeks to destroy a believer's assurance of salvation with his weapons of doubt and discouragement. It shields you from mental and emotional attacks. The battlefield is the mind.

Since Paul addresses believers, putting on the helmet of salvation cannot refer to receiving Christ as Savior. The only ones who can take up any piece of God's armor, and the only ones who are involved in this supernatural struggle against Satan and his demon forces, are those who are already saved. It is clear from Paul's reference to the helmet as "the hope of salvation" (Isa. 59:17).

The helmet is related to salvation, indicating that Satan's blows are directed at the believer's security and assurance in Christ. The two dangerous edges of Satan's spiritual broadsword are deceit, discouragement, and doubt.

To discourage us, he points to our failures, sins, unresolved problems, poor health, or whatever else seems negative in our lives. To make us lose confidence in the love and care of our heavenly Father. Satan's most disturbing attack against believers tempts them to believe they have lost or could lose their salvation. Few things are more paralyzing, ineffective, or miserable than insecurity. Jesus said, "These things I have spoken to you, that you may have peace" (John 16:33). How can a doubting heart have peace?

How can a person who lives in continual uncertainty about his salvation be comforted by such promises when he is not sure they apply to him or will always apply to him? If he loses his salvation, he loses those promises as well. How could such a person not have a troubled and fearful heart? Those promises would be mocked to him. But although Satan may seriously damage a Christian's feelings about his salvation inspired doubt, his salvation itself is eternally protected, and he need not fear its loss.

Knowing Satan's plan, Jesus assures us that "all that the Father gives Me shall come to Me, and the one who comes to Me I will certainly not cast out, and this is the will of Him who sent Me, that of all that He has given Me I lose nothing but raise it on the last day" (John 6:37, 39). No situation, no failure, shortcoming, or sin, no matter how serious, can cause either Jesus or His Father to disown a person who is saved.

Satan wants to curse the believer with deceit and doubts but the Christian can be vital in God's promises of eternal salvation in Scripture (John 6:37-39; 10:28-29; Romans 5:10; 8:31-39; Phil. 1:6; 1 Peter 1:3-5). Security is a fact; assurance is a feeling that comes to the obedient Christian (1 Peter 3:1-10).

The helmet of salvation is that great hope of finishing salvation that gives us confidence and assurance that our present struggle with Satan will not last forever and we will be victorious in the end. We know the battle is only for this life, and even a long earthly life is no more than a split second balanced to eternity with our Lord in heaven. We are not in a race we can lose.

"*The sword of the Spirit*": As the sword was the soldier's only weapon, God's Word is the only needed weapon, considerably more powerful than any of Satan's.

The Greek term refers to a slight weapon eight inches long. It was used both protectively to fend off Satan's attacks and to help destroy the enemy's strategies. It is the truth of Scripture.

"*Of the Spirit*" can also be interpreted "by the Spirit" or as "spiritual," meaning to the nature of the sword rather than its source. From the situation, we know that it is a spiritual weapon to be used in our struggle against spiritual enemies. As the Spirit of truth (John 14:7), the Holy Spirit is the believer's resident truth Teacher, who teaches us all things and brings God's Word to our remembrance. The sword of the spirit is, first, a defensive weapon, competent in averting an opponent's blows. It is the believer's supreme weapon of defense against the onslaughts of Satan.

However, unlike the shield, which gives extensive and general protection, the sword can avert an attack only if handled accurately and expertly. It must evade the enemy weapon exactly where the thrust is made.

When Satan tempted Jesus in the wilderness, His defense for each temptation was a passage of Scripture that correctly undermined the devil's word (Matthew 4:4, 7, 10). The Christian who doesn't know God's Word well cannot use it well. Satan will consistently find out where we are ignorant or confused and attack us there.

Christians who rely simply on their experience of salvation and their feelings to get them through are in danger of spiritual danger. They get into countless conceding situations and fall prey to immeasurable false ideas and practices simply because they are ignorant of the certain teachings of Scripture.

The helmet covers the head. It is just saying that our minds have stayed on the fact that we are saved. A reason waited upon the Lord will not be convinced with false religion made appealing to man's mind. Our weapon is the Word of God. Spirit here is the Holy Spirit. The Word of God is made clear to our understanding by the teaching of the Holy Spirit. When Jesus baptizes in the Holy Spirit, it sets us on fire to carry the accurate Word of God to all who will receive it. The two most potent things today are the spoken and the written Word of God. Win battles for God with the Word of God. The genuinely relinquished my life is the life committed to aggressive, confronting, and unreserved obedience to all of God's commands. The Word of God is so powerful it transforms men from the realm of falsehood to that of truth, from the realm of darkness to that of light, and from the realm of sin and death to that of righteousness and life. It changes sadness into joy, despair into hope, inactivity into growth, childishness into maturity, and failure into success.

No believer has an excuse for not knowing and understanding God's Word. Every believer has God's own Holy Spirit within Him as his divine teacher of God's sacred Word. Our only task is to submit to His instruction by studying the Word with sincerity and commitment. We cannot plead ignorance or inability, only disregard and neglect.

Ephesians 6:18 "Praying always with all prayer and supplication in the Spirit, and watching thereunto with all perseverance and supplication for all saints;."

The general character of a believer's prayer life:

- ❖ *"All prayer and supplication"* focuses on diversity.
- ❖ *Praying always"* focuses on the frequency (Rom. 12:12; Phil. 4:6; Thess. 5:17)
- ❖ *"In the Spirit"* focuses on submission, as we line up with the will of God (Romans 8:26-27)
- ❖ *"Watching thereunto"* focuses on the manner (Matt. 26:41; Mark 13:33)
- ❖ *All perseverance"* focuses on persistence (Luke 11:9; 18:7-8).
- ❖ *"All saints"* focuses on the objects (1 Sam. 12:23).

All the while that we are fighting in the girdle of truth, the breastplate of righteousness, the shoes of the gospel of peace, the shield of faith, the helmet of salvation, and the sword of the Spirit, we are to be in prayer. Prayer is the very spiritual air that the soldier of Christ breathes. It is the all-persistent tactic in which warfare is fought.

"Praying" is grammatically linked to "stand." Without prayer, God's armor is deficient to achieve victory. Prayer is essential. "Always means "on every occasion" when Satan attacks. "In the Spirit" signifies that with the Spirit's help, such prayer for divine aid is to be made. We are to be involved in all kinds of prayer and every suitable form of prayer. We may pray publicly or privately; in loud cries, in whispers, or silently; deliberately and planned or spontaneously; while sitting, standing, kneeling, or even lying down; at home or in church; while working or while traveling; with hands folded or raised; with eyes open or closed; with head bowed or erect.

Like the Old Testament, the New Testament mentions many forms, circumstances, and postures for prayer but stipulates none. Jesus prayed while standing, while sitting, while kneeling, and quite probably in other positions. We can pray wherever we are and in whatever situation. "Therefore, I want the men in every place to pray" (1 Tim. 2:8), Paul said. For the faithful, Spirit-filled Christian, every place becomes a place of prayer. To always pray is to live in continual God-consciousness. Everything we see and experience becomes a kind of prayer, lived in deep awareness of and surrendering to our heavenly Father. To obey this exhortation means that, when we are tempted, we hold the temptation before God and ask for His help. When we experience something good and beautiful, we immediately thank the Lord for it. When we see evil around us, we pray that God will make it right and be willing to use Him to the end. When we meet someone who does not know Christ, we pray for God to draw that person to Himself and use us to be a faithful witness.

When we encounter trouble, we turn to God as our Deliverer. In other words, our life becomes a continually ascending prayer, a perpetual conversing with our heavenly Father. To always pray is to constantly set our minds "on the things above, not on the items on earth (Col. 3:2). To pray in the Spirit is to pray in the name of Christ, to pray consistent with His nature and will. To pray in the Spirit is to pray in concert with the Spirit, who:

"Helps our weakness; for we do not know how to pray as we should, but the Spirit Himself intercedes for us with groanings too deep for words, and He who searches the hearts knows what the mind of the Spirit is because He intercedes for the saints according to the will of God" (Romans 8:26-27).

As the *"Spirit of grace and supplication"* (Zech. 12:10), the Holy Spirit continually prays for us; for us to pray rightly is to pray as He prays, joining our pleas to His and our will to His. It is to line up our minds and desires with His mind and desires, which are consistent with the intention of the Father and the Son.

To be *"filled with the Spirit"* (Eph. 5:18) and walk in, his highest power must be made to pray in the Spirit because our prayer will then be in harmony with His. As we submit to the Holy Spirit, obeying His Word and relying on His leading and strength, we will be drawn into close and deep fellowship with the Father and the Son.

To pray appropriately also involves praying particularly. "Whatever you ask in My name," Jesus promised, "that will I do, the Father may be glorified in the Son. If you ask Me anything in My name, I will do it" (John 14:13). God answers prayers to put His power on display. And when we do not pray in detail, He cannot answer exactly and thereby clearly display His passion and His love for His children.

As young children often do, "God bless the whole world" is not to pray. We must think about certain people, specific problems, and actual needs, and then pray about those things precisely and earnestly to see God's answer and offer Him our thankful praise.

Most Christians never get serious about prayer until a problem arises in their own life or in the life of someone they love. Then they are motivated to pray intently, precisely, and constantly. Yet that is the way Christians should always pray. Compassion for the problems and needs of others, especially other believers who are facing trials or hardships, will lead us to pray for them "night and day," as Paul did for Timothy (2 Tim. 1:3).

"Watching thereunto" means "being vigilant in the very matter" of prayer. We are to pray not just for themselves but also "for all saints." Spiritual combat is both an individual and corporate matter.

"Supplication" here means petition. So many people do not realize the power of praying in the Spirit. When you have run out of words to say, you let the Spirit of God pray through you for the matter.

God knows just exactly what to pray for. Not only are we to petition God for ourselves in prayer, but for all the believers in Christ called saints.

Paul seeks their prayers on his behalf that he may "boldly" or plainly "make known the gospel" and "speak" it "boldly" as it ought to be preached. Paul does not ask for prayer for his wellbeing or physical comfort in the imprisonment from which he wrote, but for boldness and faithfulness to continue declaring the gospel to the unsaved no matter what the cost.

Ephesians 6:19 "And for me, that utterance may be given unto me, that I may open my mouth boldly, to make known the mystery of the gospel,"

Paul did not beg or pray on his behalf so that his ankles, raw and sore from his shackles, might be healed. Or that he might be freed from prison and suffering. His deep concern was that utterance might be given unto me in the opening of my mouth to make known the mystery of the gospel with boldness.

When Satan tempted him to keep quiet about Christ, he wanted God's help to be bold and faithful to proclaim the gospel. He wanted help in his battle against Satan, and he prayed with his brothers and sisters at Ephesus to pray toward that end.

Paul also needed the prayers of fellow believers because he was a leader. Our enemy knows that the sheep will scatter when he strikes the shepherd.

This "*utterance*" of speaking boldly about the mystery of God is speaking as an oracle of God. The Lord says through your mouth. Each time a minister preaches, they should be allowing God to speak to the people through them. The boldness comes when you realize that you are not talking in your might but God speaking through you.

Ephesians 6:20 "For which I am an ambassador in bonds: I may speak boldly, as I ought to speak."

Even in prison, it was important to Paul that he would make known the mystery of the gospel with boldness because it was his own boldness that attracted the Praetoria Guard to the gospel and inspired courage in other witnessing Christians. Even when he requested prayer for himself, Paul's purpose and intention were selfless, to further the gospel, encourage other believers, and glorify his Lord.

An ambassador does not communicate his view but is a glorified message delivery service for whoever sent him. Paul says I can be bold because this is God's message to you, not my message.

CHAPTER 22

The Valley of Decision

Revelation 17

The Valley of Decision

- ❖ *Women: God's people, the church*
- ❖ *Beast: world order, kingdom, nations*
- ❖ *Season: seven mountains*
- ❖ *Harlot: unfaithful church/ counterfeit church*
- ❖ *False Prophet: false doctrine*
- ❖ *Church Colors: purple and scarlet*
- ❖ *The Scarlet Woman and the Beast*
- ❖ The woman is a great city: "The woman you saw is the great city that rules over the kings of the earth" (Rev. 17:18). Many have taken this to mean that the woman symbolizes the capital city of Antichrist's kingdom, Vatican City, which sits on seven hills or mountains.
- ❖ Rome
- ❖ Papal: Pope
- ❖ False Prophet
- ❖ Unfaithful Church
- ❖ Counterfeit Church
- ❖ Antichrist himself rules over the kings of the earth.

The Woman is:

- ❖ Mystery, Babylon the great,
- ❖
- ❖ The Mother of Harlots and the Abominations of the Earth
- ❖ World dominance

There will be one world order system before which all kings, dictators, kingdoms, and nations will be forced to bow down throughout the Babylonian religion of idolatry. No one cannot go anywhere in the world without being confronted with some impression of idolatry.

This system in the world will enslave more people in this horrible religion. It should not take some by surprise that this prostitute woman is the world's religious system as a city.

When used figuratively, a woman is throughout the Scripture a prostitute," it represents the corrupt religious system of idolatry; indicate a spiritual or religious movement. If a good woman, it is "Jehovah's wife" or "the bride of Christ." If an evil woman, such as "a prostitute," it signifies the corrupt religious system of idolatry.

The Beast

The woman who rides the beast gets her authority from the beast; the Holy Spirit uses this explanation to show how religious Babylon and governmental Babylon are so entangled they are organized together. However, they are destroyed at different times. The prostitute is spiritual. Babylon is destroyed by the "beast and the kings of the earth," who "hate the prostitute" and kill her.

The Antichrist/ False Prophet: Pope

The Antichrist fulfills Satan's lifetime dream to get people to worship him. He is destroyed in the middle of the Tribulation; Babylon's governmental system will be destroyed at the end when commercial, political Babylon is destroyed (Rev. 18).

"Mystery Babylon, the Mother of Prostitutes" out of the way, "all inhabitants of the earth will worship the beast, all whose names have not been written in the Book of life have its place with the Lamb that was slain from the creation of the world" (Rev. 13:8).

The Vision of the Woman – Ten things describe this woman:

- The great prostitute.
- Who sits on many waters?
- With her, the kings of the earth committed adultery
- The inhabitants of the world intoxicated with the wine of her adulteries
- A woman sitting on a scarlet beast
- Dressed in purple and scarlet: High Priest Garments
- Glittering with gold, precious stones, and pearls
- She held a golden cup in her hand, filled with abominable things and the filth of her adulteries
- On her forehead: Mystery Babylon the Great, the Mother of Prostitutes, and the Abomination of the Earth.
- She was drunk with the blood of the saints, those who bore testimony to Jesus.

The angel's interpretation of this vision, we are not doing business with a mere human being, for no one woman can commit fornication with the kings of the earth, nor can a woman be "drunk with the blood of the saints, the blood of those who bore testimony to Jesus."

There scriptures Chapters 17 and 18, the judgment of God on a system, empire, or city called Babylon the Great (17:5); the seventh vial (16:17). The "great whore" is *"BABYLON THE GREAT."* Chapters 17 and 18 show her "judgment."

The "waters are the various peoples and nations of the earth. She "sits upon" them in the sense that she has worldwide influence. Her harlotry and "fornication" refer to physical immorality or spiritual adultery. Idolatry and religious apostasy (Isa. 1:21; 23:16-17; Jer. 2:20-37; 13:27; Ezek. 16:15-43; Hosea 2:5; Nahum 3:4). The "kings" and "people of the earth" have opened their arms to her influence.

A Counterfeit Sanctuary

These great evils, which have damned the souls of millions by substituting counterfeit solutions to natural human problems that would ordinarily lead a person to God, will all be destroyed at the end of the Tribulation period. Chapter 17 describes the coming judgment of God on the religious system that has enslaved the human race in superstitious darkness for centuries.

Revelation 17 is the destruction of the religious Babylon one world order about the center of the seven years after the Antichrist declares himself to be God and no longer needs the One World Religion.

The next chapter is about the destruction of the commercial, political Babylon at the end of the Great Tribulation. In ancient days Satan appeared to make Babylon the capital of this evil operation. From this headquarters was started false religion, humanity's attempt for self-government in defiance of God's will, and city dwellings for commercial and social purposes contrary to God's command to "be fruitful and increase in number and fill the earth" (Gen. 1:28).

The woman is a great city: "The woman you saw is the great city that rules over the kings of the earth" (Rev. 17:18). Many have taken this to mean that the woman is the capital city of Antichrist's kingdom; for Antichrist: Pope himself rules over the kings of the earth.
Revelation 17:1 "And there came one of the seven angels which had the seven vials, and talked with me, saying unto me, come hither; I will show unto thee the judgment of the great whore that sits upon many waters:"

"*Seven angels*": These angels' links with the vial bowl, judgments, which extend to the second coming of Christ. Chapters 17 and 18 bring attention to one characteristic of those vial judgments, the decision of Babylon. The decisions already explained are known as targeting the final world system.

"*Great whore*": Babylon- Prostitution regularly signifies idolatry or religious apostasy (Jer. 3:6-9; Ezek. 16:30ff; 20:30; Hosea 4:15; 5:3; 6:10; 9:1). The daughters of Babylon churches are also represented as harlot cities.

"*Sit on many waters*": This is the sovereign power of the harlot. A ruler seated on a throne, ruling the waters, signifies the world's nations.

This "*whore*" here is not a literal woman. In Hosea, his wife, who was a whore, was speaking of Israel. Here, this "whore" is speaking of the *idolatrous church.*

Roman Catholics Church

"*Sit upon many waters*" speaks of enormous groups of people. It is an unfaithful church. This is the apostate church. God calls it the harlot church, the church that is not faithful to God, the worldly church. While claiming to be Christian, this church observes many excuses to conform to the beast and the corrupt world system. The one-world religion will appear after the church Christians have been raptured "*One World Order Religion.*"

The church has compromised with the world and is no longer a chaste virgin in the sight of God. We believe that a large portion of that church falls into this category today. Worldliness has crept into our churches. The sad thing is that if she repented, God would take her back, but she would not repent.

The Bride of Christ is called a city and is the church that has not compromised. The other side of that is the harlot. It is also called a city but is evil because of compromise and the apostate church in Rome, but the apostate in many other churches. The waters let us know that this apostate church is throughout the multitudes of people.

Revelation 17:2 "With whom the kings of the earth have committed fornication, and the earth's inhabitants have been made drunk with the wine of her fornication."

Kingdoms and nations: kings, presidents, senators, congress, ambassadors, apostles, pastors, bishop, teachers, ministers, prophets' governors, majors, etc. have committed fornication": The harlot will partner herself with the world's political leaders.

Fornication here does not refer to idolatry. All the world rulers will be absorbed into the empire of Satan's false Prophet.

"Wine of her fornication": The harlot's pressure will extend beyond the world's rulers to the rest of humanity.

The world's people are being swept into the intoxication and sin of a false system of religion. This universal apostasy, unfaithfulness to God, does not affect all classes of people. This unfaithfulness is from the rich and influential political leaders to the very poor.

The way a drunken person has no earthly idea what he is doing, this apostate company is so carried away with the world that they do not realize the terribleness of what they are doing. God will judge this idolatrous church. Judgment begins at the house of God first.

Revelation 17:3 "So he carried me away in the spirit into the wilderness: and I saw a woman sit upon a scarlet-colored beast, full of names of blasphemy, having seven heads and ten horns."

"In the spirit": The Holy Spirit transports John into the wilderness, a deserted, lonely, and desolate wasteland, to give him a better understanding of the vision.

"A woman": The harlot Babylon.

"Scarlet colored beast": The Antichrist who for a time will support and use the false religious system to affect world unity. Then he will assume political control. Scarlet and Purple is the color of luxury, splendor, and royalty.

- ❖ "Full of names of blasphemy": Because of his self-deification (Dan. 7:25; 11:36; 2 Thess. 2:4).
- ❖ "Having seven heads and ten horns": Antichrist's political alliances
- ❖ This "wilderness" means the world.
- ❖ This "scarlet colored beast" shows evil world power.

The woman sits upon this beast, which means that her power comes from this evil beast (Revelation 18:2); it supports her. This woman: The Church has decided to trust the management of this world over God's power.

- ❖ Seven implies spiritually complete, ten implies world government, and horns symbolize power.

We can easily see that she is on top of this beast; she guides it but receives her support from the beast. The word "scarlet" can be very good or very evil. It isn't kind. The great evil blasphemy that this woman-church has committed is spiritual adultery (watering down or changing the Word of God). The elegant clothing and jewelry of the "woman" show her wealth and attractiveness, but her activities are filthy and abominable to God. Her mystery name *is BABYLON THE GREAT"*.

A great deal of the world's idolatry can be traced back to historical Babylon (Gen. 11:1-9), *the mother-child cult of Semiramis-Tammuz* (Jer. 44:16-19; Ezek. 8:9, 14), other cultures as *Ashtaroth-Baal, Aphrodite-Eros, Venus-Cupid, and Madonna-Child*. The fountainhead of idolatry, *Babylon the harlot is the* **MOTHER OF HARLOTS AND ABOMINATION OF THE EARTH.** The harlot has killed many of God's "saints" and Christian "martyrs" throughout the ages and will do so again during the Tribulation period.

Revelation 17:4 "And the woman was arrayed in purple and scarlet color, and decked with gold and precious stones and pearls, having a golden cup in her hand full of abominations and filthiness of her fornication:"

The Roman Catholic priest is the only one arrayed in Purple and scarlet. *"Purple and scarlet"*: Royalty, nobility, and wealth colors. The woman is a prostitute who successfully plied her trade and became extremely wealthy. They are the most affluent church in the world.

"Decked" Prostitutes often dress in fine clothes and precious jewels to charm their victims (Prov. 7:10). Babylon's religious harlot is no different, adorning herself to lure the nations into her grasp.

"A golden cup": Still another evidence of the harlot's great wealth (Jer. 51:7), but the filthiness of her immorality defiles the pure gold. Just as a prostitute might first get her victim drunk, so the harlot system deceives the nation into committing spiritual fornication with her.

This "fornication" is spiritual adultery or compromise with the world. God will tolerate most anything except the worship of someone else or something else. It has to do with the watering down of Jesus, who he is. Ancient Babylon is a foreshadow of this future Babylon. The harlot will do what actual Babylon did in the past:

- Oppress God's people, and
- Propagate a false religious system.
- Semiramis: Ishtar and Isis, both Nimrod's wife and mother, were worshiped as the "mother of god" and a *"fertility goddess"* because she had to be extremely fertile to give birth to all the pagan incarnate gods that represented Nimrod.
- Cush begat Nimrod: he began to be a mighty one in the earth.

The one-world order religion as defined (Rev. 17:4) is most revealing: "The woman dressed in purple and scarlet." As published in national magazines in the Vatican Council, you will have observed that the bishops and cardinals wore purple and scarlet robes.

You will also see that the pope and other church leaders are "glittering with gold, precious stones, and pearls." They hold "a golden cup in their hand, filled with abominable things and the filthiness of their adulteries." These abominable things and adulteries are the idolatry and worship of gods other than Jesus Christ. In Rome, all manner of idols can be seen in the headquarters of the Roman Church. More costly surroundings can scarcely be found than in the Vatican.

The Catholic Church is often decorated this way, including all the apostate churches; Protestants and Catholics are called Babylon's daughters. The people are sitting on a church pew but not being the bride of Christ. There are some in all churches, but the church in Rome most assuredly. You can see great masses of gold, silver, and jewels. Usually, when a church building is decked out like this, it is in an area where there is miserable poverty.

- ❖ "Purple": this was in the church because purple means godliness. It was a false godliness.
- ❖ Golden cup": this is inside the church because gold figuratively means the purity of God.
- ❖ We know this "cup" belonged to God. To means that the world's sins have been brought into the church.

This "fornication" is spiritual adultery or compromise with the world. God will tolerate most anything except the worship of someone or something else. It has to do with the watering down of Jesus.

Revelation 17:5 "And upon her forehead was a name written, ***MYSTERY, BABYLON THE GREAT, THE MOTHER OF HARLOTS AND ABOMINATIONS OF THE EARTH.***"

- ❖ "*Forehead*": It was customary for Roman prostitutes to wear a headband with their name (Jer. 3:3), parading their wretchedness for all to see. The harlot's forehead is adorned with a 3-fold title narrative of the world's final false religious system.
- ❖ "*Mystery*": A New Testament mystery is truth hidden but in the New Testament revealed (Matt. 13:11; Eph. 3:4-5).

Spiritual Babylon's identity was revealed- the Roman catholic church. Thus, it has been manifested in the world for years under the demon of deception.

❖ *"BABYLON THE GREAT"*: This Babylon is Babylon's historical, geographical city.

❖ MOTHER OF HARLOTS": All false religion stems ultimately from Babel, or Babylon (Gen. 11).

Just as God marked the 144,000 with the name of the Father, and just as the bride of Christ is marked with the name of Christ, we see here this group marked on the forehead. This name alone makes you know how evil and worldly this church is.

666

❖ 6- Satan
❖ 6- Beast: Mark- hand or forehead
   a. 6- man
      1. Roman Catholics church
      2. Most affluent church in the world
      3. The Harlot of Babylon
      4. False Doctrine
      5. Counterfeit church
      6. Unfaithful church
      7. The daughters of Babylon churches of the world.
      8. Bitcoins: new money
❖ 6-Papal: Pope
      1. Antichrist
      2. False Prophet
      3. Son of the devil
      4. Cast down God Sanctuary

This worldly part of the church, though nominally Christian, is yet more faithful to the world than to God. The church that pretends to be Christian and is not does more to cause harm than those worldly people who claim to be lost. The worldly church always persecutes the faithful church. This evil in the church is an abomination to God. The mystery is the demon of deception.

The Counterfeit Representation the Roman Catholics church has committed for centuries are:

- ❖ *Altar of Sacrifice*: The priest from the church offers forgiveness, confession, and penance
- ❖ *Laver*: Infant sprinkling and pouring
- ❖ *Table of Showbread:* Church took access to God's Word away. Put superstition and tradition above God's Word.
- ❖ *Altar of Incense*: Earthly priests intercede for the people
- ❖ *Seven Branch Candlestick*: Priests, not the people, are responsible for witnessing. Priests used force and compromise to win converts
- ❖ *Ark of the Covenant*: Modified God's law to remove the seventh-day Sabbath to Sundays (Deut. 5- Ten Commandments). Understand the difference between the True Church and the Counterfeit Church.

A Counterfeit Sanctuary

The Pope and priests have magnified himself even to the prince of the host, and by him, the daily sacrifice was taken away, and the place of his sanctuary was cast down. And a host was given him against the daily sacrifice because of transgression, and it cast down the truth to the ground; and practiced, a prospered (Daniel 8: 11-12}

The True Church Representation – God's Church:

- ❖ *Altar of Sacrifice:* All appropriate sacrifices of Christ for the forgiveness of sins.

- ❖ *Laver*: Baptism- Cleansing by personal choice to repent and accept Christ.
- ❖ *Table of Showbread*: Bible- Word of God, spiritual nourishment
- ❖ *Altar of Incense*: our prayers and Christ's intercession
- ❖ *Seven Branch Candlesticks*: Witness of Christ through his body (Church) on earth.
- ❖ *Ark of the Covenant*: Law of God; Sabbath- Friday evening to Saturday evening. (Deut.5- Ten Commandments). Understand the difference between the True Church and the Counterfeit Church.

The fountainhead of idolatry, Babylon the harlot is the MOTHER OF HARLOTS AND ABOMINATIONS OF THE EARTH; the harlot has killed many of God's saints and Christian martyrs throughout the ages and will do so again during the Tribulation period.

Revelation "17:6 And I saw the woman drunken with the blood of the saints and the blood of the martyrs of Jesus: and when I saw her, I wondered with great admiration."

The blood of the saint's martyrs of Jesus": The first group is Old Testament saints. The second is New Testament saints, an unimportant difference between the "witnesses," or martyrs, of the Tribulation. John's point is that the harlot is a murderer. The false religion has killed millions of believers over the centuries, and the final wrong system will be far more deadly than any that preceded it.

The faithless part of the church is guilty of the blood of the saints. In Matthew 12:20, Jesus says, "He that is not with me is against me." This watered-down church is causing significant problems for those sold out to God. We know Rome had a great deal to do with the death of the martyrs and even had a hand in crucifying Jesus.

The Jews church of that day had even more, to do with the crucifixion of Jesus. However, the most blame for His death must be placed on us. Sin put Jesus on the cross. He went to the cross to crucify sin. His sacrifice stopped us from being a servant to sin.

Out of it all, with the Bible as their guide, how could these people get so far away from God and still occupy a pew? The answer is quite simple. They never read or study their Bible themselves. They allow someone else to read it and tell them what it says. However, much of the problem lies at the shepherd's feet. So many preachers are overlooking the need for the spiritual growth of their people.

The 34th chapter of Ezekiel says God will take the sheep away from the shepherds that do not care for them. **_Shepherds BEWARE!_** We are not to be as concerned with "our" needs as we are with "our people" needs.

From the last few scriptures above, we see that this is speaking of Rome and the Catholic Church, who have brought the compromise. Even more than that, it is speaking to individuals in all churches who have compromised themselves. 2 Timothy 3:5. "Having a form of godliness but denying the power thereof: from such turn away. "A person is claiming to be a Christian on the outside, but who is not on the inside. It's so easy to point to someone else, but we should examine ourselves as well.

"Scarlet woman" and a "Beast." The Beast as an empire goes through four stages, the beginning of the Tribulation period":

- ❖ It existed in the form of the ancient Roman Empire.
- ❖ Since the fifth century, it has not existed as an empire and will not live again until the Antichrist gains worldwide authority during the Tribulation period.
- ❖ It "shall ascent out of _the bottomless pit_," that is, Satan will raise the Antichrist as his false messiah and give him worldwide rule (Rev.11:7; 13:3-4)
- ❖ The Antichrist cast into "_perdition_," the lake of fire (Rev,19:20). Unbelievers will "_wonder_" in amazement at this revival of the power and glory of the Roman Empire (Rev.13:3).

Revelation 17:7 "And the angel said unto me, wherefore didst thou marvel? I will tell thee the woman's mystery and the beast that carried her, which hath the seven heads and ten horns."

"*Mystery*": Not that Babylon is a false system of religion, because that is already known, but that the beast will fully support the harlot and exercise vast influence over the whole earth.

The Vision of the Beast – Five details explaining the beast, are given:

- ❖ Blasphemous names (verse 3)
- ❖ Had seven heads (verse 3)
- ❖ And ten horns (verse 3)
- ❖ The prostitute rides it (verse 7)
- ❖ The beast was, and is not, and will come out of the *bottomless pit (Abyss)* and go to his destruction (verse 11).

The Bible student will immediately recognize this beast even before examining the angel's interpretation. In the first place, the beast (Rev. 13) and doubtless signifies what all beasts used to represent: either a king or a kingdom that opposes God's will.

When John sees the great prostitute, he is "greatly astonished?" Parts of this vision have been familiar to John, for it is evidently the same beast as described (Rev. 13). The angel introduces his justification with the words, "This calls for a mind with wisdom" (verse 9), which indicates that only someone with the wisdom of God in the Word of God can understand this vision.

Revelation 17:8 "The beast that thou saw was and is not and shall ascend out of the bottomless pit and go into perdition: and they that dwell on the earth shall wonder, whose names not written in the book of life from the foundation of the world when they behold the beast that was and is not, and yet is."

- ❖ "The beast": This term refers to a king and kingdom.
- ❖ And shall ascend" the Antichrist's false resurrection (Rev. 13:3-4; 12-14; Rev.13:3).

❖ *"Out of the bottomless pit"*: After his "resurrection," the Antichrist will become possessed by a great demon from the abyss (Rev.13:1, 3).

❖ This mark indicates that the power given unto this group comes from the bottomless pit.

Here it is speaking of the restructuring of the old Roman empire. The old Roman empire has been transformed by the ten common market nations in Europe today. These "ten horns" are these ten common market nations. The headquarters for these ten nations is in Rome. In 1954 the Ten Member States were: Belgium, France, Germany, Greece, Italy, Luxembourg, Netherlands, Portugal, Spain, and the United Kingdom.

❖ *"Go into perdition"*: Eternal destruction (Rev.11; Matt. 7:13; John 17:12; Phil. 1:28; 3:19; 2 Thess. 2:3; Heb. 10:39; 2 Peter 2:3; 3:7, 16). It is the lake of fire, the place of Antichrist's destruction (19:20).

❖ "Book of Life": The role of the elect, written in eternity past by God (Rev. 3:5). Only the elect will escape the Antichrist's deception (Matt. 24:24).

"From the foundation of the world" (Rev.13:8; 2 Tim. 1:9; Titus 1:2), "long ages ago". A common phrase (Matt. 13:35; 25:34; Luke 11:50; John 17:24; Eph. 1:4; Heb. 4:3; 9:26; 1 Peter 1:20), referring to God's pre-creation plan.

"perdition" means ruin, loss, or damnable. This Roman Empire was in great power; it fell and then revived again in the ten nations. It is a wonder how Berlin was divided into two parts after World War II. It was done so the line of the old Roman Empire would be the same. Of course, the governments of the U.S. and Russia did not know why they did this, but it established the old territory anyhow.

❖ "The beast that thou saw.

"Whose names were not written in the book of life." The false religious system of the end times will be compelling and popular among the unsaved. Still, those who have committed themselves to Christ will understand that anything idolatrous is not of God.

In The reformation period, The Archbishop of Canterbury was one of the most influential religious leaders in the English reformation. He has killed during the reign of Mary I. The three monarchs during this period were Henry VIII, Edward VII, and Mary I. (Unknown, Canonical Books, 12th Century).

Whatsoever the church teaches you out of the canonical books of the bible, believe it. But if they teach you anything different that is not agreeable with the bible, think that they don't leave you fast to the sound and certain doctrine of God's infallible word (Unknown, Canonical Books, 12th Century).

Angels of the Seven Churches

The mystery of the seven stars you saw in my right hand and the seven golden lampstands.

The Seven Stars: are the angels of the seven churches, and The Seven Lampstands, which you saw, are the seven churches (Rev. 1:20).

Revelation 2:

❖ To the angel of *the church of Ephesus,* write, *The Loveless Church*: Nevertheless, I have this against you, that you have left your first love. Remember, therefore, from where you have fallen, repent and do the first works, or else I will come to you quickly and remove your lampstand from its place -unless you repent. To him who overcomes, I will give to eat from the Tree of Life, which is amid the paradise of God.

Let him hear what the Spirit says to the churches who have an ear. (Holy Bible, KJV, 2012).

❖ And to the angel of *the church in Smyrna* writes, *The Persecuted Church:* I know the blasphemy of those who say they are Jews and are not but are a *synagogue of Satan.* Do not fear any of those things which you are about to suffer. Indeed, the devil is about to throw some of you into prison, that you may be tested, and you will have tribulation for ten days. Be faithful until death, and I will give the crown of life. The second death shall not hurt him who overcomes.

Let him hear what the Spirit says to the churches who have an ear. (Holy Bible, KJV, 2012).

❖ And to the church's angel in Pergamos write, The Compromising Church: I know your works, where you dwell, where Satan's throne is. But I have a few things against you because you have; they're those who hold the doctrine of Balaam, who taught Balak to put a stumbling block before the children of Israel, to eat things sacrificed to idols, and commit sexual immorality. Repent, or else I will come to you quickly and fight against them with the sword of my mouth. Let him hear what the Spirit says to the churches who have an ear. To him who overcomes, I will give him a Whitestone and a new name written on the stone that no one knows except him who receives it.

Let him hear what the Spirit says to the churches who have an ear. (Holy Bible, KJV, 2012).

❖ And to the church's angel *in Thyatira,* write *The Corrupt Church*: Nevertheless, I have a few things against you because you allow that woman Jezebel, who calls herself prophetess, to teach and seduce my servants to commit sexual immorality and eat things sacrificed to idols. And I gave her time to repent of her sexual sin, and she did not repent. I will cast her into a sickbed and those who commit adultery with her into great tribulation unless they repent of their deed.

Let him hear what the Spirit says to the churches who have an ear. (Holy Bible, KJV, 2012).

Revelation 3:

❖ And to the angel of *the church in Sardis*, write *The Dead Church:* Remember therefore how you have received and heard; hold fast and repent, therefore, if you do not watch, I will come upon you as a thief, and you will not know what hour I will come upon you. You have a few names even in Sardis who have not defiled their garments, and they shall walk with Me in white, for they are worthy. He who comes shall be clothed in white garments, and I will not blot out his name from the Book of Life, but I will confess his name before My Father and before His angels.

Let him hear what the Spirit says to the churches who have an ear. (Holy Bible, KJV, 2012).

❖ And to the church's angel *in Philadelphia*, write, *The Faithful Church:* Behold, I am coming quickly! Hold fast what you have, that no one may take your crown. He who overcomes, I will make him a pillar in the temple of My God, and he shall go out no more. I will write on him the name of My God and the name of the city of My God, the New Jerusalem, which comes down out of heaven from My God. And I will Write Him My new name.

Let him hear what the Spirit says to the churches who have an ear. (Holy Bible, KJV, 2012).

❖ And to the angel of *the church of the Laodiceans* write, *The Lukewarm Church*: Because you say, I am rich, have become wealthy, and need nothing- and do not know that you are wretched, miserable, poor, blind and naked- I counsel you to buy from Me gold refined in the fire, that you may be rich; and white garments, that you may be clothed, that the shame of your nakedness may not be revealed; and anoint your eyes with eye salve, that you may see. As many as I love, I rebuke and chasten. Behold, I stand at the door and knock. If anyone hears My voice and opens the door, I will come into him and dine with him, and he with Me. I will grant to sit with Me on My Throne to him who overcomes, as I also overcame and sat down with My Father on His throne.

Let him hear what the Spirit says to the churches who have an ear. (Holy Bible, KJV, 2012).

References:

KJV, The Holy Bible, (2012). (ALL RIGHTS RESERVED). *The Holy Bible KJV*. Knoxville, TN 37921: Power Publishing Corporation.

NKJV, The Holy Bible, (2012). *Spiritual Warfare Bible*. Lake Mary, Florida 32746: Charisma House.

Unknown. (12th Century). *Old and New Testaments*. Rome: Canonical Books.

ABOUT THE AUTHOR

I was born in New York State, but raised in Quincy, Florida. After graduating from High School at James A. Shanks in 1975 I enlisted in the Army. I decided to enter the United State Army from 1975-1995 I serviced twenty years as a Staff sergeant as an Ammunition Inspector. I retired in 1995. I gave my life to the Lord in 1990, before Desert Shield and Desert Storm. She is charter member of the Women's Military Service of America Memorial Foundation in Washington, D.C. and a Gulf War/ Desert Shield and Desert Storm veteran.

She is a veteran Consultant that help other veteran known how to file their claims at their liaison lawyers American Legion, Disable veterans, and Foreign Affairs. I find it a joy to be enlisted in God's Army now. It has taken God's strength and power that has kept me all these years. She loves to write, travel, and spend time with family. She now lives in Indianapolis, Indiana with her husband Darren Smith, and she has two daughters grown Sabrina and Michele, and four grandsons: Kamari, Lucas, Terrance, and Jonathan; and brother Cedric Forks. She also has two Dogs: Princess BB-Miniature Schnauzer, Cherri: Siberian Husky both are females.

www.ingramcontent.com/pod-product-compliance
Lightning Source LLC
Chambersburg PA
CBHW021001150626
46549CB00012BA/316

* 9 7 9 8 9 8 9 9 9 5 0 5 4 6 *